13

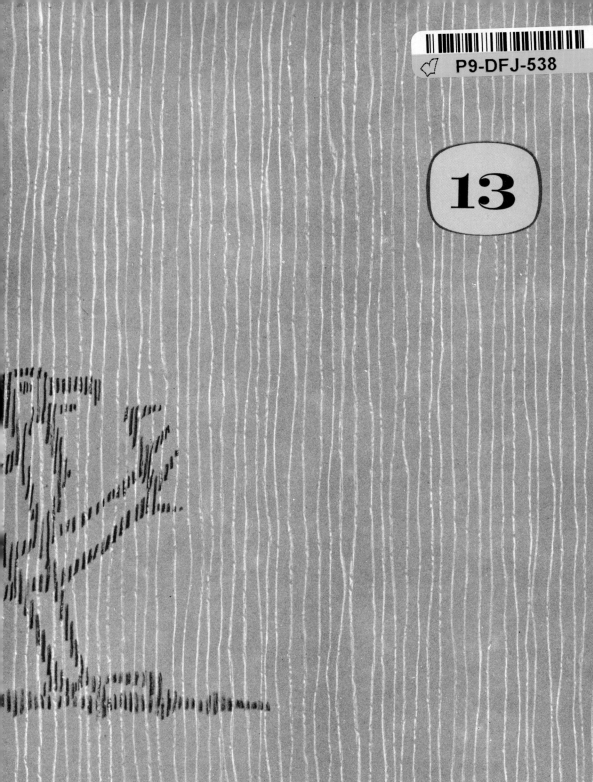

SPECIAL CONSULTANTS

THE GOLDEN TREASURY OF
KNOWLEDGE

VOLUME
13

OF SIXTEEN VOLUMES CONTAINING 420 BASIC
ARTICLES WITH 2500 ILLUSTRATIONS AND MAPS

Margaret Bevans
EDITOR-IN-CHIEF

Joanna Aldendorff
EDITORIAL CONSULTANT

Clifford Junceau
PROJECT CONSULTANT

Tom Torre Bevans
DIRECTOR

EDITORIAL STAFF
Renée Algrant · Doris Ballard · Richard Keigwin
I. W. Klein · Morgan Larkin · Henry Mins
Carol Z. Rothkopf · Peter Share

PRODUCTION STAFF
Rosalie Barrow · Frank Bologna · Ken Braren
Rosemary Gutwillig · Alan M. Heicklen
Yvonne Charles Johnson · Harris Lewine · Alice Lupo
Peter Marks · Tomaso Puliofito · Bruce Ross · Loretta Trezzo

COVER BY Ray Pioch

GOLDEN PRESS · NEW YORK

About
VOLUME 13
and
how it relates to other volumes

In Volume 13 you will meet an American humorist and a carefree island people. You will learn about dramas in ancient Greece, the first American post office, a famous valley of roses, and the invention of the needle. You will also learn how matter is formed and how goods are exchanged.

Some subjects that interest you will have many aspects that are covered in articles in other volumes. For example, STONE AGE MAN may make you want to learn more about prehistoric tools or eating habits. It is easy to pursue any subject by looking up the particular topic in the index in Volume 16.

And almost any article may interest you in a related topic. THE MIGHTY ATOM—ITS STRUCTURE may lead you to THE MIGHTY ATOM—ITS POWER, to CHEMISTRY, or to ALBERT EINSTEIN in other volumes. AIR TRANSPORT may interest you in THE FIRST AIRSHIPS or THE WRIGHT BROTHERS. GEOGRAPHY could lead you to another science, GEOLOGY, in another volume.

In reading any volume of the *Golden Treasury of Knowledge,* you will find a world of new and fascinating information.

CON

PAGE

The Polynesians
An island people who lead simple lives and have mysterious origins — 1064

Mark Twain
Famous lecturer, writer, and humorist, who was once a river pilot — 1068

Gorillas
Apes more like men than monkeys in appearance and intelligence — 1072

The Balkans
A European peninsula constantly overrun by neighboring countries — 1074

Lenses
The different types, their uses, and how they bend light rays and heat rays — 1078

The Ancient Greek Theater
The stage and arena, the actors, and the types of plays performed — 1082

Air Transport
Planes and airports, and their importance in travel and trade — 1086

The Deserts of America
Where they are found, how they were formed, and what animals and plants live in them — 1088

T E N T S

Japan

A chain of mountainous islands, and a modern industrial nation   1092

Icebergs

Dangerous floating islands of ice, and modern ways of discovering and tracking them   1096

How the Bodies of Animals Are Protected

Coats that adapt to climates, and coats that change color   1099

Stone Age Man

The first fire, first art, first tools, and first villages   1103

Plant Sensitivity

Why plants grow toward light and their roots grow toward water   1106

Northern Africa

A land of barren desert, historic crossroads of conquering nations   1108

Insect Bites and Stings

How they are inflicted, the dangerous ones, and the merely annoying kinds   1113

Animals of the Tropical Forest

From acrobatic monkeys to poisonous and nonpoisonous reptiles   1115

Germany

From the start of the Holy Roman Empire to today's divided nation   1118

Jet and Rocket Engines

The different types, the principles behind them, and how they work   1123

Trade and Commerce

The traffic of goods, its different forms, and its history   1126

Geography

Its history and major branches, and the relationship of the earth to man   1130

How Fish Breathe

The structure and development of gills, and double-breathing fish   1135

The Incas

Skillful builders of a vast, rich empire, conquered by the Spanish   1138

The Mighty Atom, Its Structure

The building blocks of matter, how they combine to form the elements   1142

Colonial America

The people, their styles of life, occupations, and communication   1146

See page 1149 for a time chart which will show how periods of history relate to one another and at what time many of the events in these articles took place.

The Polynesians

Polynesia means many islands. These islands are in the Pacific Ocean and are enclosed in the lines of an imaginary triangle, each of whose sides is more than 4,500 miles long. Polynesia stretches in a rough triangle from the Hawaiian Islands in the north almost to New Zealand in the south. The eastern boundary is formed by islands a few thousand miles off the coast of South America. The Polynesian people live on such islands as the Marquesas, Samoa, Tonga, Cook, New Zealand, Hawaii, Easter Island, Ellice, and Society, as well as many others.

There are only about 300,000 purebred Polynesians left in the world. In the 18th century, Captain James Cook, who visited some of the Pacific islands, reported that there were some 400,000 Polynesians in the Hawaiian Islands, and 300,000 more in Tahiti. Since then the population has decreased. Many Polynesians, such as those in Hawaii, intermarried with other races. Others died when European settlers arrived on the islands and brought new diseases and new customs to which the Polynesians could not adapt themselves.

Nobody is sure where the first Polynesians came from. They were a race of great sailors and were capable of traveling thousands of miles in their long outrigger boats. They were known to have war canoes manned by as many as 300 men. They had no instruments for navigation, but guided themselves by the stars. They could tell something about currents from plants floating on the ocean, and about the winds from the flights of birds. They had many skills that helped them to find their way among the tiny, isolated islands in the middle of the Pacific Ocean.

The Polynesians are physically different from the other Pacific islanders. They are tall and light skinned. Some have straight hair and

The Polynesian who does not live in the city lives by fishing and by picking coconuts, bananas, breadfruit, and other products of his fertile islands. Houses are made of wood and have thatched roofs.

some have curly hair. They are classed among the Caucasoid races of man, and some people believe they were Caucasians who migrated from Asia in the days before recorded history. In language, there are many similarities between Polynesian and Indonesian. There are also similarities in customs. But many other Polynesian customs resemble those of the South American Indians, and there are some archeologists who speculate that the Polynesians may be linked with Indians of Peru and Chile who sailed from the west coast of South America into the Pacific.

The Polynesian culture is very old. A great deal of their history is preserved in songs and dances. Historians have tried to guess at Polynesian history from talking with the people. But each island has its own legends and its own version of how it was settled. On Easter Island, for instance, tablets of wood inscribed with a mysterious writing have been found.

They might tell a good deal about the early Polynesians, but unfortunately nobody can read these tablets now.

When European explorers discovered the Pacific islands, the lives of the Polynesians began to change. Gradually the Europeans found that the islands were valuable and they sent settlers and missionaries there. By the 19th century, many of the islands were owned by differ-

As dancing is an important part of their lives, Polynesians learn to dance when they are children.

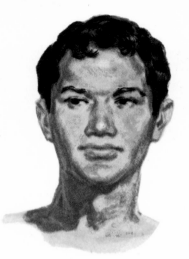

Polynesians are handsome, light skinned, and well built. The origin of the people is unknown.

Children search for mollusks and shells in the warm water that surrounds the islands.

ent countries and, although their status was changed by the two World Wars, most of them are still under the mandate of various European governments or are owned by them.

The Polynesians themselves resisted all the attempts of Europeans to make them work on plantations. They did not care about owning property or want many possessions. They liked to swim and fish and dance and sing. Life was slow and easy in the fertile islands and the Polynesians did not see why it should be otherwise. The Polynesians believed in great social freedom. Unlike other Pacific tribes, they considered the position of women equal to that of men. Sometimes women ruled their communities as chieftains.

Polynesian religion was based on worship of ancestors. They also believed there were spirits in many things in nature. Some things were taboo—forbidden—but for the most part the people lived very freely. The Christian missionaries converted most of the Polynesian people. However, they still make tapa cloth and paint it with ancient religious stories, and carve wooden statues of their old gods which have now become legends.

Except in the cities, Polynesian life has remained much the same. The people fish and swim and create works of art. They use coconuts for food and drink, and the shells for cups and dishes. They also eat bananas, breadfruit, sweet potatoes, and yams. They build their houses on platforms to keep them from being flooded after a rain. The walls of the houses are made of wood, and the roofs are thatched with palm leaves.

The Polynesians dress themselves in *pareus,* simple cloths which they wind around their bodies. For dance ceremonies, which play a great part in Polynesian life, they often wear grass skirts, kilts made of leaves, garlands of woven flowers, and other elaborate ornaments. In Hawaii the missionaries of the 19th century persuaded the women to wear a long, loose garment known as the Mother Hubbard, or muumuu. Many different versions of this nightgownlike dress, brightly colored and decorated, are now worn in Hawaii.

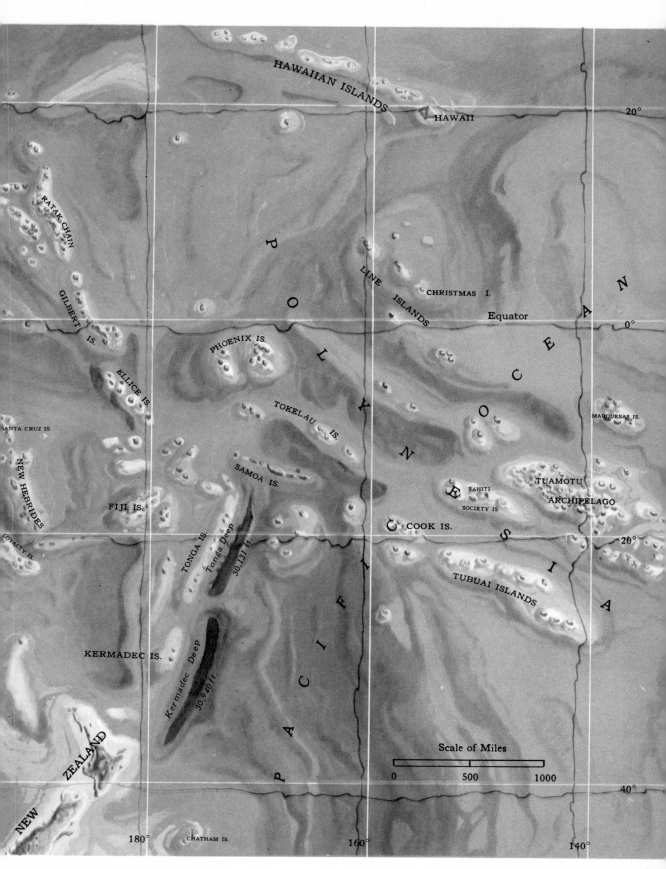

HAWAIIAN ISLANDS

HAWAII

20°

RATAK CHAIN

P
O
L
Y
N
E
S
I
A

LINE ISLANDS

CHRISTMAS I.

Equator

0°

GILBERT IS.

PHOENIX IS.

ELLICE IS

MARQUESAS IS.

SANTA CRUZ IS.

TOKELAU IS.

NEW HEBRIDES

SAMOA IS.

TAHITI

TUAMOTU
ARCHIPELAGO

FIJI IS.

SOCIETY IS

LOYALTY IS

COOK IS.

20°

TONGA IS.

Tonga Deep

30.131 ft.

TUBUAI ISLANDS

KERMADEC IS.

Kermadec Deep

30,940 ft.

P
A
C
I
F
I
C

O
C
E
A
N

NEW ZEALAND

Scale of Miles

0   500   1000

40°

180°

CHATHAM IS.

160°

140°

1067

Mark Twain

More than 100 years ago in the small town of Hannibal, Missouri, a boy watched the steamboats make their way through the treacherous channels of the Mississippi River. He watched the crewmen measuring the depth of the water. Often, as they passed, he heard them shout to the pilots, "By the mark, twain!" The mark was the second six foot knot on their measuring lines. It meant that their boats were traveling safely in 12 feet of water.

The boy's name was Samuel Langhorne Clemens. The world knows him as Mark Twain. For, when he grew up and became a writer, he took the famous old river cry as his pen name.

Mark Twain is the United States' best known and best loved humorous writer. He was born in 1835 in the inland town of Florida, Missouri. When he was four, his parents moved to the bustling river port of Hannibal. There he

Mark Twain drew upon his boyhood experiences in growing up along the Mississippi for two of his best known books, The Adventures of Tom Sawyer *and* The Adventures of Huckleberry Finn.

grew up among the many colorful characters—pilots, gamblers, adventurers—who made their living along the Mississippi. There he heard and stored away in his memory many tales about the river and its people. Young Sam Clemens had little formal education. He spent a few years in an old-fashioned school that had no separate grades. But the teeming river life provided an exciting schooling of its own.

With other boys, Sam built rafts and explored the Mississippi's many shoals and hidden places. His lively imagination made even the most commonplace event exciting to him. Long afterwards, his recollections of those years of growing up in Hannibal formed the background for his two most famous books, *The Adventures of Tom Sawyer* and its sequel *The Adventures of Huckleberry Finn.* They have been translated into almost every language and are sold in almost every country in the world. Many of the incidents involving Tom Sawyer and Huck Finn actually happened in real life to young Sam Clemens and his boyhood friends.

The Clemens family was very poor, and at the age of 12 Sam went to work for his brother, who was a printer. Sam learned to set type for a small newspaper, the Hannibal *Journal*. This was his early introduction to journalism and writing. Later he tried his hand at printing jobs in distant cities. But life along the Mississippi called him back. At 22 he made a boyhood dream come true—he became a river pilot. He worked on freighters and passenger steamboats up and down the Mississippi, more than 1,000 miles each way. He learned to know every snag, every shifting sandbar, every dangerous crosscurrent. *Life on the Mississippi* is his account of five years of exciting experiences on the river.

When the Civil War broke out, steamboating came to a halt on the river. Some pilots turned to soldiering, others joined the great trek to the Far West. Sam Clemens tried both. For a few weeks he served as a volunteer in a Confederate company, but army life didn't appeal to him, and he resigned to accompany his brother to Nevada.

Nevada was still a territory. Great new gold and silver deposits had been discovered there. Sam Clemens went by stagecoach across the Great Plains and the Rockies to try his luck at gold prospecting. He lived in rough mining camps. He went through sandstorms and blizzards to stake claims both in the desert and in the mountains. At night around campfires he

As a young man, Sam Clemens lived in the mining camps of the Nevada Territory. While a reporter for the Virginia City paper, he wrote many humorous sketches and first assumed his famous pen name Mark Twain.

Mark Twain wrote popular travel letters for several California newspapers. His letters from a Mediterranean tour, commissioned by the Alta California *in San Francisco, were collected together to become Twain's first significant book,* The Innocents Abroad.

entertained his fellow prospectors with funny stories. Although Sam didn't find any gold or silver, prospecting rewarded him with a wealth of rich experience which he wrote about later in a hilarious book called *Roughing It.*

In Virginia City, Nevada, he became a reporter. He wrote humorous pieces for the local newspaper, and it was there that the pen name Mark Twain first appeared in print. He wrote about the colorful characters he met in mining camps and the exaggerated yarns they told. His humor was broad and down-to-earth, and soon readers all over the West were laughing heartily at this new author who understood them so well.

One of his earliest short stories, *The Celebrated Jumping Frog of Calaveras County,* was printed in many newspapers. Almost overnight Mark Twain's writing became known all over the country. A few years later his travel book, *Innocents Abroad,* made him world famous.

Soon, in addition to writing, Mark Twain began to deliver humorous lectures and readings from his own works, and audiences roared with laughter at his dry wit. His career as public entertainer lasted for years, and he toured the entire country many times.

For a period of 40 years Mark Twain was the most widely read author in the United States. Volume after volume appeared—modern satires, humorous essays, romances such as *The Prince and the Pauper,* and a serious novel about Joan of Arc. As he grew older, he became more concerned with philosophy than with his earlier broad humor.

Although he lived in many cities, he spent a great part of his life in Hartford, Connecticut, with his wife and daughters. His one son died as a baby. Writing and lecturing took up only part of his great energy. He was an active partner in a book publishing firm, and it was Mark Twain who persuaded ailing ex-President Grant to publish his memoirs. He also traveled widely. In Europe, wherever he went, crowds flocked to see and hear this celebrated American. He died in 1910 at the age of 75 at Stormfield, a country home he had built in Redding, Connecticut.

Gorillas

The gorilla is one of the anthropoid, or man-like, apes. The others are orangutans, gibbons, chimpanzees, and siamangs. Many of the physical characteristics that make man different from other mammals are also found in the anthropoid apes.

Among these characteristics are 32 teeth, lack of a tail, a broad, flat breastbone, finger-nails, an appendix, and a wide pelvis. The

brains of man and the great apes are similar, but man's is more fully developed. The great apes act almost like men. In intelligence they are far beyond monkeys and in appearance closer to man than monkeys. But there are differences.

Gorillas have much longer arms than men. A man's armspread is usually about the same as his height. An adult five and a half foot go-

A family of gorillas in an equatorial forest. Gorillas live in the forested parts of tropical Africa.

rilla may have an armspread of eight feet. Its legs, however, are weak, so that when it swings on tree branches, it uses only its arms. Gorillas have not only grasping fingers, but also grasping toes. Adults generally walk on all fours, resting on the soles of their feet and the knuckles of their hands. They also sit, squat, and stand erect.

Apes were first known before the birth of Christ, but gorillas were not described scientifically until the middle of the 19th century. They are native to equatorial West Africa and the eastern Congo region. They normally live in forests and jungles and eat vegetables and fruits. They travel in bands made up of immediate families—perhaps a male, two females, adolescent young, and infants.

Their growth is remarkably rapid. A young gorilla in a zoo in Berlin, Germany, weighed 33 pounds when it arrived. After one year it weighed 65 pounds, after another year it

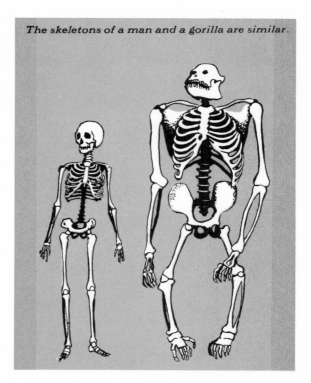

The skeletons of a man and a gorilla are similar.

weighed 100 pounds, in another two years it weighed 200 pounds, and when it was seven or eight years old, it weighed 640 pounds. A very large male is usually about five and a half feet tall with a chest that measures 60 inches. It sometimes weighs more than 600 pounds, but its usual weight is about 400. Females are much smaller and lighter. Gorillas are black or iron gray. Young animals have hair on their bodies, but old males become bald on their chests and upper backs.

Gorillas look ferocious, but they are not aggressive. When faced with an intruder, a gorilla may shriek and howl and pound its chest, but if this does not drive the intruder away, the gorilla itself usually leaves.

Gorillas eat such enormous quantities of food that they must keep moving from one place to another to find it. At night the females and the younger members of the family climb into a tree to sleep. They usually build beds for themselves in the lower branches of the tree. But the adult male cannot climb trees because it is too heavy. It builds its nest on the ground and sleeps with its back against the tree.

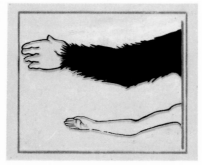

The arm size of a gorilla compared with the arm size of a man of the same height

A large adult male gorilla may weigh enough to balance four grown men on a see-saw.

The Balkans

The continent of Europe has three peninsulas that project southward from the central land mass. The Iberian peninsula is occupied by Spain and Portugal. The Italian peninsula is occupied by Italy. The Balkan peninsula on the southeastern corner of the continent is occupied by all or part of the six Balkan states— Yugoslavia, Bulgaria, Rumania, Albania, Greece, and Turkey. The peninsula includes only the portions of these states that lie south of the Danube and Sava rivers.

The Italian and Iberian peninsulas are separated from the main part of Europe by mountains. But the mountains of the Balkan peninsula do not form a protective frontier, so wave after wave of invaders has swept into the Balkans from the east, north, and west.

Before the time of the Roman Empire the Balkan peninsula was inhabited by barbarian tribes. The Romans conquered parts of the area, and they were replaced by Slavic peoples, many of whom are still there. During the 14th century the Turks moved westward and eventually conquered most of the peninsula. Starting

ALBANIA
AREA: *10,629 square miles*
POP: *1,500,000*
CAPITAL: *Tirana*
RELIGIONS: *Moslem, Orthodox Christian,
Roman Catholic*
LANGUAGES: *Ghegish, Toskish*
MONETARY UNIT: *Lek (2¢)*

BULGARIA
AREA: *42,796 square miles*
POP: *7,722,000*
CAPITAL: *Sofia*
RELIGION: *Eastern Orthodox*
LANGUAGE: *Slavonic*
MONETARY UNIT: *Lev (14.7¢)*

GREECE
AREA: *51,246 square miles*
POP: *8,173,000*
CAPITAL: *Athens*
RELIGION: *Greek Orthodox*
LANGUAGE: *Greek*
MONETARY UNIT: *Drachma (3.33¢)*

RUMANIA
AREA: *91,584 square miles*
POP: *18,059,000*
CAPITAL: *Bucharest*
RELIGION: *Rumanian Orthodox*
LANGUAGE: *Latin base with traces of French,
Greek, Slav, and Turkish*
MONETARY UNIT: *Lev (16.67¢)*

TURKEY
AREA: *296,500 square miles*
POP: *26,880,000*
CAPITAL: *Ankara*
RELIGION: *Moslem*
LANGUAGE: *Turkish*
MONETARY UNIT: *Lira (11.11¢)*

YUGOSLAVIA
AREA: *98,766 square miles*
POP: *18,397,000*
CAPITAL: *Belgrade*
RELIGIONS: *Serbo-Orthodox, Roman Catholic,
Moslem, Protestant*
LANGUAGES: *Slovene, Macedonian, Serbo-Croat*
MONETARY UNIT: *Dinar (.33¢)*

in the early 19th century the Turks were slowly pushed back into Asia by the Balkan peoples, with some help from their European neighbors. Today only a small part of the peninsula still belongs to them. But in some countries they once controlled, the people are still Moslems, as in Albania. There, more than two thirds of the population is of the Moslem faith.

When the Turks were forced out of the Balkans, various European powers wanted to take their place. At different times the Germans, the French, the English, the Austrians, the Italians, and now the Russians have controlled large parts of the area. The Balkan peninsula has been called the Powder Keg of Europe, because it seemed that a small quarrel in the Balkans could easily start a general European war. This was actually true in 1914. The assassination of Archduke Francis Ferdinand, at Sarajevo—now in Yugoslavia—triggered World War I.

In World War II most of the Balkans was overrun by the German armies. When the Russians defeated the German invaders, Albania, Bulgaria, Rumania, and Yugoslavia became Communist satellites. In 1948 Yugoslavia broke away from Soviet control and proclaimed itself an independent Communist country. Its president, Marshal Tito, insisted that neither the Russians nor the Americans could dictate to him. At present, Albania, Bulgaria, and Rumania are allied with Russia, and Greece and Turkey are allies of the United States, with Yugoslavia in the middle.

Albania is the smallest of the Balkan countries. It is mountainous and a little larger than Maryland. Its Albanian name means Rocky Land, and Albanians call themselves Rock Dwellers. About 1,500,000 people live in Albania, and they are probably more isolated than any other people in Europe. Most of them live in small villages or lonely houses in the valleys between the high mountains. They have very little contact with the outside world. Even Tirana, the capital, with a population of about 65,000, is visited by few Europeans.

The Bulgarian parliament meets in the city of Sofia.

Bulgaria is on the eastern side of the Balkan peninsula. Since ancient times it has been a meeting place between East and West, so the land has been fought over for hundreds of years. The capital of Bulgaria, Sofia, has about 500,000 inhabitants.

The high tableland of Bulgaria is very fertile. Vast amounts of wheat are grown there. When the Turks controlled the Balkan peninsula, this northern part of Bulgaria supplied most of their grain.

The evzones are a special Greek infantry corps. One of their duties is acting as a royal guard.

Through the center of Bulgaria run the Balkan mountains. While some of them are quite high, there are low passes and many roads through them. In southern Bulgaria, Mt. Musala and Mt. Eltepe are nearly 10,000 feet high, the highest peaks in the Balkans. Northeast of the mountains is a stretch of rolling country called the Valley of Roses. This sheltered valley has an ideal climate for growing roses. The blossoms are picked in the early morning while they are still wet with dew. They are then distilled until they yield a precious oil, called attar of roses, which is used in making perfumes. Bulgaria is the most important producer of this oil. As much as 2,000 pounds of rose petals are needed to make one pound of attar of roses!

Greece was the first Balkan country to win back her freedom from Turkey. The Greek War of Independence was fought from 1821 to 1829. The German army conquered Greece in World War II. After the war the Communists tried unsuccessfully to seize the government. The Americans, by means of the Truman Doctrine and the Marshall Plan, helped the Greeks to retain their independence. Greece is now a constitutional monarchy, and the present king is Paul I.

Greece is a land of many islands with a coastline greater than that of either the Iberian or Italian peninsulas. The deep indentations not only prevent any point of land from being further than 50 miles from the sea, but also form natural harbors that have enabled Greece throughout her history to maintain an internationally important merchant marine fleet.

Athens, the capital, was one of the most splendid cities of the world in ancient times. It is still the largest city in the Balkans, with a population of nearly 1,500,000.

After Athens, the most important Greek city is Salonika. It was already a great military and commercial port in Roman times. Many of the inhabitants of Salonika are descended from Sephardic Jews from Spain, who fled their country during the religious persecutions of the 16th century. After 400 years in Greece they still speak a language that sounds more like Spanish than Greek.

Rumania is on the borders of countries which have been fighting each other for hundreds of years. It has been a frequent victim of these wars.

The Danube river forms the border between Rumania and Bulgaria for 284 miles, but it flows through Rumania for the last 190 miles of its journey to the Black Sea. It is one of the great rivers of Europe. The delta is largely uninhabited. The land is swampy, and there are clouds of anopheles mosquitos, which cause malaria. The Danube deposits about 3,000 cubic feet of sediment in the Black Sea every minute. The Danube is navigable for small vessels all the way to Ulm, in western Germany, a distance of nearly 1,500 miles from its mouth.

The Carpathian mountains make a great arc through central Rumania. These mountains are very old and they have been worn smooth by time. Grazing land is sometimes found even on their peaks. The capital of Rumania is Bucharest. With a population of 1,250,000, it is the second largest city in the Balkans.

Turkey is a large country, but the portion of it on the Balkan peninsula is quite small. The rest of the country is in Asia. 90 percent of the Turks live in Asian Turkey, but their largest city is in European Turkey. It is Istanbul, on the west side of the Bosporus. It has a population slightly smaller than that of Bucharest. Istanbul was called Constantinople when it was the capital of the Ottoman Empire. Before that its name was Byzantium, and it was the capital of the Eastern Roman Empire.

The small part of the Balkan peninsula that Turkey still owns is all that is left of her European possessions, which once included all the present Balkan countries and southeast Europe as far as Vienna.

Yugoslavia is the largest of the Balkan countries and covers an area about equal to that of Wyoming. Its population is almost 18,400,000. Its territory joins Italy at Trieste. It also shares borders with Austria and Hungary, so that it has more contact with western Europe than any other Balkan country except Greece.

This bridge across the Mat River is in Albania.

Yugoslavia is divided into three major regions. On the Adriatic coast is Dalmatia. The coastline is broken, with many limestone cliffs and islands. The central zone, which occupies most of the country, is mountainous. The northern plain, divided in half by the Danube, is the only large level area in Yugoslavia. It is very fertile.

On the Dalmatian coast, about 50 miles north of the Albanian border, is one of the largest natural harbors in the world, the Bay of Kotor. The winding fiordlike inlet, which is 20 miles long, could hold hundreds of ocean liners at one time. But no ocean liners ever stop there, because Kotor is not on any major sea lane.

Most of the Yugoslavs are Serbs, Croats, Macedonians, and Slovenes. The Montenegrins, who live in the mountains near the Albanian border, are probably the tallest people in Europe.

The capital of Yugoslavia is Belgrade, with a population of just over 500,000. Belgrade lies at the junction of the Sava and Danube rivers. Since it controls the river traffic on the Danube, it has probably seen more battles within its walls than most European fortresses. And it has probably changed hands more often than any other capital city in the world.

Lenses

Lenses are made of a transparent substance such as glass or quartz through which light can pass easily. They are usually circular in shape and have either two curved surfaces or one curved and one flat surface. Lenses are used to correct defective eyesight, to take photographs, to project moving pictures, to observe very small objects, to look at things that are too far away to be seen by the naked eye, and for many other purposes.

No one knows when lenses were first discovered. It was certainly a long time ago, for lenses have been found in Roman tombs which are at least 2,000 years old. Some of the work on Greek, Egyptian, and Roman objects of art is so fine that the artists must have had magnifying lenses. The fact that a lens can collect the rays of the sun to start a fire has been known for many centuries. Burning glasses, as they were called, were used by the ancient people of Asia Minor.

When light rays pass through a lens they are bent. The way in which they are bent depends on the shape of the lens. There are two main shapes of lenses, convex and concave.

A convex lens is thicker in the center than at the edges. When light rays pass through a convex lens they are bent inward and toward one another. An ordinary magnifying glass is a convex lens.

A concave lens is thinner in the center than at the edges. Light rays going through a concave lens are bent outward and away from one another. Nearsighted people have concave lenses in their eyeglasses.

If an electric bulb is put in front of a convex lens, the light rays go off in all directions from the light bulb, traveling in straight lines. Some of the rays enter the lens and emerge on the other side. The rays are still going in straight lines, but they are not going in the same direction as before because they have been bent by the lens. Only one light ray is not bent, the one that passes through the exact center of the lens.

The farther the light rays are from the center of the lens, and the closer to its edge, the more they are bent. The rays from the light bulb that pass through the very edge of the lens are bent the most. Therefore, all the rays that pass through the lens, since they started from a single point—the light bulb—meet in a point on the other side of the lens. If we place a screen at that point, we will see reproduced on it the image of the light bulb.

Of course a light bulb is not a single point of light. But it is made up of single points of light. The rays from each one are collected by the lens and gathered into a single point on the other side of the lens. All the images of all the points, taken together, make up the image of the light bulb, and this is visible on the

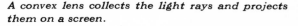

A convex lens collects the light rays and projects them on a screen.

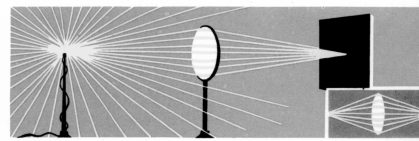

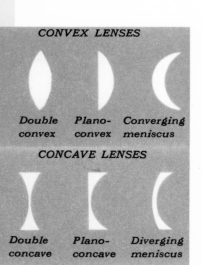

CONVEX LENSES

Double convex

Plano-convex

Converging meniscus

CONCAVE LENSES

Double concave

Plano-concave

Diverging meniscus

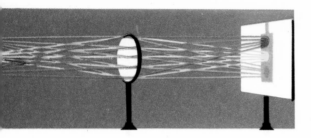

The image of the object that is formed on a screen by a convex lens is upside down.

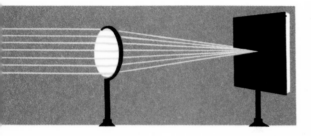

The point at which all the light rays come together after passing through a lens is called the focal point.

screen. The rays from the top of the object go to the bottom of the image, and the rays from the bottom of the object go to the top of the image. Thus, the image on the screen is upside down.

If the lighted object is very far away from the lens, the rays that come from it are nearly parallel. The sun, for example, is a lighted object that is so far away that we can consider its rays to be parallel. After passing through the lens, the rays come together at a single point. This is called the focal point, or the focus (f), of the lens.

When the sun's rays are brought together by a lens, it is not only the light rays that are made to converge. The sun's heat rays are also collected by the lens and gathered together at the focal point. This produces a concentration of heat that may be strong enough to ignite a piece of wood or paper.

The distance between the center of a lens and its focal point is the focal distance (F) of the lens. The focal distance is the most im-

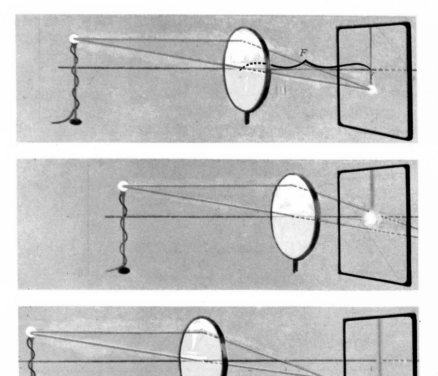

If a screen is set exactly at the meeting point of the light rays, the image is sharp. It is in focus.

If a screen is closer to a lens than the meeting point of the light rays passing through the lens, the image is blurred. It is out of focus.

The image is also blurred if a screen is farther away from the lens than the meeting point of the light rays passing through the lens, which is called the focal point. The image is out of focus again.

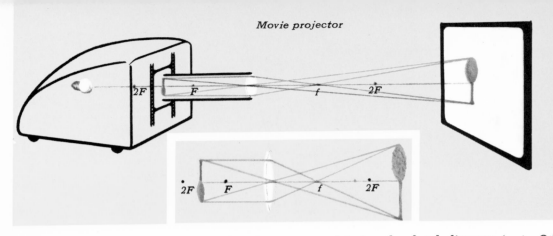

portant feature of any lens. Every lens has a particular focal distance which distinguishes it from all others and indicates the lens's magnifying power. It defines the uses to which the lens can be put.

Using the light bulb, lens, and screen, we leave the light and the lens in the same position. If we move the screen back and forth we can see that in only one position of the screen is the image of the light bulb sharp and clear. This happens only when the screen is at the focal point of the lens.

There are two basic uses to which lenses can be put. They can be used to project an image or to throw a beam of light, either into the air or on a screen. They can also be used to gather a beam of light coming from an object —in other words, to look through.

An example of the first basic use is the movie projector. Here the lighted object is the picture of a tree on the film. It is important to place the film between the focus of the lens

and twice the focal distance (   ). Otherwise the image could not be focused. On the screen side of the lens, the image appears at a point beyond twice the focal distance. The image will be inverted, and the film must be inserted upside down so that the image will be rightside up. Since it is not convenient to move the screen back and forth, the lens in the projector is moved back and forth to focus the image on the screen.

Another example is the lighthouse lens. Here the object, in this case a powerful light, is placed exactly at the focus of the lens. This situation is just the opposite of the one where we found the focal distance of the lens. There the sun's rays came in parallel as far as the lens and were gathered to a point. Now the rays from the light start at the focal point and are thrown out parallel after passing through the lens. No image is formed, but the rays are concentrated in a beam that can be seen at great distances. If the light is not placed ex-

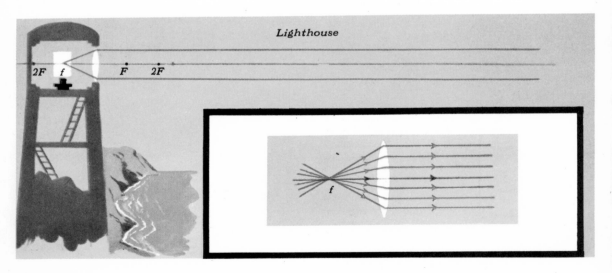

Lighthouse

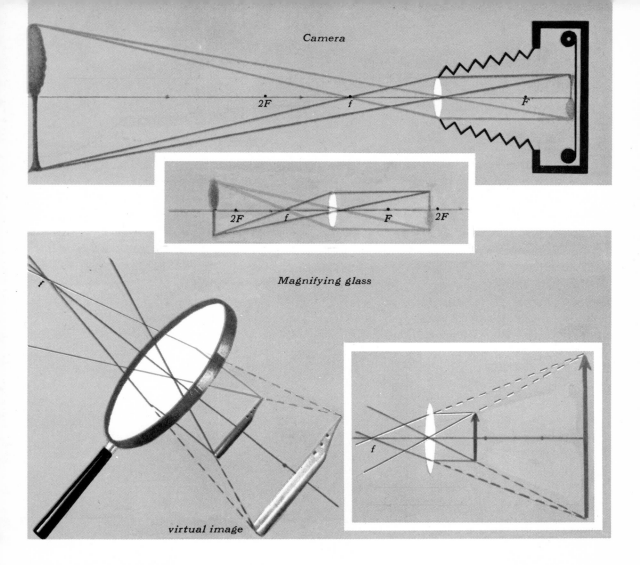

Camera

2F   f   F

2F   f   F   2F

Magnifying glass

f

virtual image

f

actly at the focal distance, the rays of light will be scattered and will not be visible far away.

An example of the second basic use is an ordinary camera. Here the lighted object must be more than twice the focal distance from the lens. The image is thrown onto the film inside the camera. The image is upside down, and it is smaller than the object. The film must be placed somewhere between the focal point and twice the focal distance. This situation is the opposite of the movie projector. Again, since it is not convenient to shift the position of the film, the lens in the camera is moved back and forth to achieve perfect focus.

Another example of the second basic use is the ordinary magnifying glass. Here the object is placed between the lens and the focal point. The rays of light coming from the object converge at the eye, which is at the opposite focal

point of the lens. But the eye does not see that the rays of light have been bent by the lens. It seems to the eye that the rays have come straight from the object. This means that the object appears to be farther away and bigger than it is. The eye does not see the real image of the object; it sees a virtual image of it. By using combinations of several lenses the image of the object can be magnified many hundreds of times.

Eyeglasses alone are a great boon to the human race. They add 20 years or more of usefulness to most people's eyes. Contact lenses that fit directly over the lens of the eye are used by some people. There are many other uses to which lenses are put, from the 40-inch lens in the telescope at the Yerkes Observatory, in Wisconsin, to a tiny lens, only 1/16 of an inch in diameter, in modern microscopes.

Ancient Greek Theater

On a hillside in Epidaurus in Greece are the ruins of one of the drama's first homes, a 2,200 year old theater. You can still see the stone seats around two thirds of a large circle on the ground, where the plays were staged. This circle was called the orchestra, the Greek word for dancing place. The old Greek theaters were similar in shape to our modern sports stadiums. Sports as well as plays were part of the Greek religious festival given every year to honor Dionysus, god of wine and fertility.

A boy or girl living in Athens in the 5th century B.C. would go to the theater with his family to celebrate this five day festival of sports, games, and plays. At first there were no real plays. A chorus sang a hymn telling stories of Dionysus and Greek heroes. The first actor was probably Thespis, who stepped out of the chorus and began to act out the story. And so, in the middle of the 6th century B.C., the drama of the Western world was born.

By the 5th century B.C. in Athens, there were plays by such great writers as Aeschylus, Sophocles, and Euripides, who wrote tragedies, and Aristophanes, who wrote comedies. Their plays were staged in outdoor theaters, the audi-

ence sitting on wooden benches on the hillside. The theaters of a hundred years later, like the one at Epidaurus, had stone seats.

At least 15,000 people could watch a play at one time, and the actors used various devices to enable them to be clearly seen and heard by everyone. The three main actors in tragedy wore high headdresses, thick-soled shoes, and large masks, whose expressions could be seen even by people seated in the back rows. Megaphones in the mouths of the masks made the actors' voices louder. Because of the heavy costumes, the actors' motions were slow and dignified. The three main tragedy actors performed as many as 11 parts. They changed costumes and masks in a long, low building on the back edge of the orchestra. This building was called a skene. The front of the skene was the background for the play's action.

Above is the Theater of Dionysus at Athens, which was the elaborate theater that developed from the outdoor stadium shown at left. In the theater the audience sat on stone benches, but in the stadium people placed wooden benches on the hillside or watched the action sitting on the grass.

Below is a mask worn by an actor in comedies.

Actors wore masks with exaggerated expressions so that people at the back could see them clearly.

A chorus of 12 to 15 singers and dancers moved in rhythm around the orchestra. They might play a group of townspeople. In Aristophanes' comedies, they played birds and frogs. In Aeschylus' *Oresteia,* they acted the Furies, three mythological winged maidens who had very ugly faces and snakes twined in their hair.

The three plays of the *Oresteia* center about the young prince Orestes, whose father, King Agamemnon, returns from the Trojan War and is murdered by his wife, Clytemnestra. With the help of his sister, Electra, Orestes kills his mother to avenge his father. For this deed his conscience and the Furies torment him. Finally, with the help of the god Apollo, Orestes is forgiven.

Tragedies like the *Oresteia* told the stories of kings of history and legend. The hero was generally a good man with one weakness which caused his unhappiness or death. Agamemnon, Orestes' father, is brave, but he is too proud. So is Oedipus, the king in Sophocles' tragedy *Oedipus Rex.*

The comedies of Aristophanes made fun of everyday life. *The Birds* is a comic fantasy about two men of Athens who believe the ways of their city to be wrong and foolish. They per-

Actors wore tall headdresses and larger than life-sized masks to make themselves more visible.

The Greek outdoor theaters were enormous and much of the audience was far from the stage.

suade the birds, which are played by a chorus of 24 people, to build an ideal city called Cloud-Cuckoo-dom.

Both tragedies and comedies were divided into five parts, with the main action preceded and followed by songs from the chorus. The parts of the tragedies were the prologue, which was the first act; the parodos, when the chorus entered; the episodes, which were the main action; the stasima, in which the chorus sang; and the exodus, the action after the last song. Comedies included the prologue, parodos, and episodes, plus an agon, which was a debate, and a parabasis, in which the chorus spoke to the audience. Both the tragedies and comedies were played at the festivals as a contest. A jury gave out prizes to the winning writer and to the winning actor.

The poetry, the people, and the stories of the ancient Greek drama have beauty and meaning for us today. The plays are still staged all over the world in many languages. Writers retell the plays, as in Eugene O'Neill's *Mourning Becomes Electra,* which is based on the *Oresteia.* And every fall at Epidaurus, in the ruins of the old Greek theater, actors perform the ancient plays just as their ancestors did over 2,000 years ago.

The main performers were versatile. They often played 10 or 11 parts, with different masks.

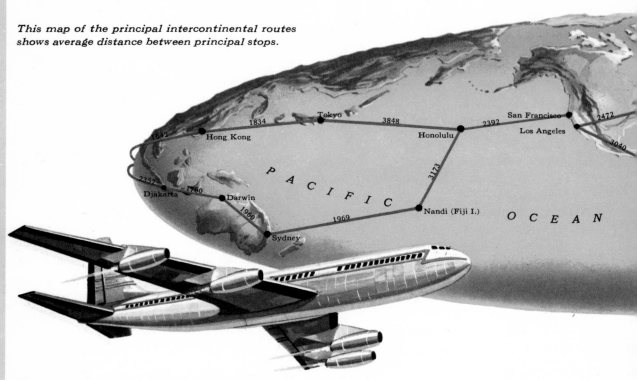

This map of the principal intercontinental routes shows average distance between principal stops.

Map labels: Tokyo, 1834, Hong Kong, 1642, 3848, Honolulu, 2392, San Francisco, Los Angeles, 2472, 3040, 3173, 2357, Djakarta, 1760, Darwin, 1960, 1969, Nandi (Fiji I.), Sydney, PACIFIC OCEAN

The Boeing 707 is one of the largest aircraft operating on international routes.

Air Transport

The airplane is the most recent form of transportation to be developed by man. It has had, however, the most rapid progress of any form of transportation. In 1903, the Wright brothers first took off from the ground in their home-made airplane. Now, thousands of airplanes carry people and freight from one part of the world to another every day.

Scientists and technicians in laboratories and manufacturing plants throughout the world are trying to discover new ways of improving the speed, comfort, and safety of to-day's airplanes. They are also concerned with additional problems, such as the most efficient kinds of airports, improving blind landings at night or in a fog, and control of aerial traffic over major cities.

The fast development of air transportation and its great popularity are due to several advantages that airplanes have. The average speed of an airplane, which is 300 miles an hour or more, is much greater than that of any other means of transportation. Average speeds on land are around 60 miles an hour, and ships average 20 miles an hour or less. The speed of an airplane is especially important for long-distance traveling, which now takes hours instead of days. It used to take five days to get to

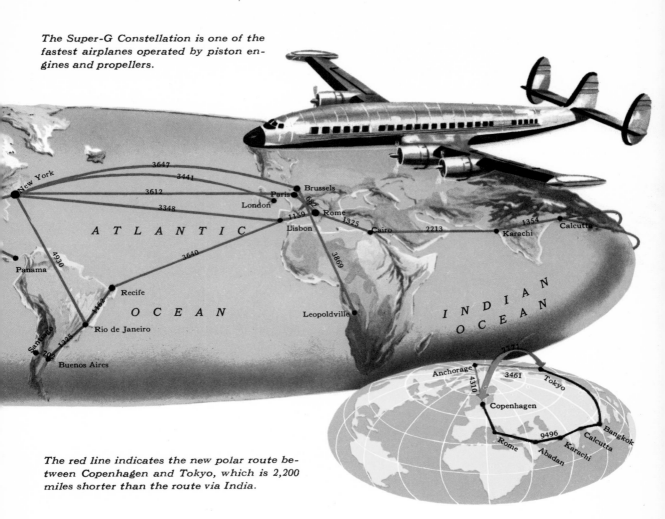

The Super-G Constellation is one of the fastest airplanes operated by piston engines and propellers.

ATLANTIC OCEAN

INDIAN OCEAN

New York 3647 3441 3612 3348 Brussels Paris London Rome Lisbon 1159 1325 Cairo 2213 Karachi 1354 Calcutta

4930 Panama 3640 Recife 3869 Leopoldville

Santiago 702 1091 Rio de Janeiro Buenos Aires

Anchorage 4310 3461 Tokyo Copenhagen Rome Abadan 9496 Karachi Calcutta Bangkok

The red line indicates the new polar route between Copenhagen and Tokyo, which is 2,200 miles shorter than the route via India.

England by ship. Today you can leave New York at breakfast time and be in London for dinner. It does take time to get to and from the airport, however, so airplanes are most useful for trips of 200 miles or more.

Another advantage of air travel is that no change of transportation is required. Formerly, a passenger going from Paris to London, or between New York and Havana, would have to travel part of the way by train and then he would have to change to a boat. An airplane ride provides the passenger with one continuous ride, except for changes at the airport.

Airplanes are also very useful in getting to isolated parts of the world. Often such places are surrounded by physical obstacles, such as deserts, mountain ranges, and frozen plains, which make overland transportation difficult or

even impossible. Also, in large countries such as Australia and Brazil, where land communications have not been well developed, the airplane can be used to carry goods and people from one part of the country to another.

In 1930 jet propulsion was first developed, and it has recently been introduced by the major airlines of the world. Jet planes are very powerful machines that weigh about 120 tons and can carry large cargoes at almost 600 miles per hour. They also fly at higher altitudes than regular airplanes, so they often avoid storms, heavy winds, and rains. They are expensive to operate, however, and for a trip of 4,000 miles they use almost 50 tons of fuel.

The rapid acceptance of jet planes does not mean that the regular piston-operated planes will disappear. They are far more convenient

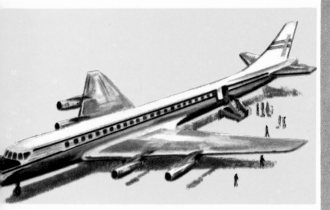

Passengers entering a four-engine jet. Such a large plane may carry 50 tons of fuel.

for shorter journeys, 500 miles or less. They are slower, but they use less fuel, they can be flown from smaller airports, and they do not need such complicated ground equipment.

Airports, which are used for take-offs, landings, and for plane storage, must be equipped with all the necessary passenger services. They have maintenance shops for repair, fuel storage tanks, and instruments for forecasting the weather. They also have radar, light signals, control towers, and the facilities to transmit and receive messages from planes in flight. Most airports stretch out for three or four square miles, and they are always being enlarged to accommodate more powerful aircraft which need longer runways.

There are about 1,000 airports in the world today, of which almost half are in the United States. Idlewild airport, near New York City, is one of the largest in the world. It covers an area of more than seven square miles and has 12 runways which can handle 360 take-offs and landings per hour. The most important European airports are in London and Paris.

Routes which go over the Arctic have been very important in recent years because of the amount of time that is saved. The line from Tokyo to Copenhagen, inaugurated in 1957, crosses the North Pole and makes a single landing at Anchorage. This flight is 2,200 miles shorter than the old route via India.

Communication between distant countries has become so fast and easy that the world seems smaller today than it did before airplanes.

Deserts of North America

A large part of the land of the United States is desert. From northern Mexico through the southwestern and western United States, the land is often arid and sandy, has little vegetation, and is inhabited by few animals. These are the desert lands of North America.

WHY THE DESERTS EXIST

A relief map of the United States partly shows why these deserts exist. The Cascade and Sierra Nevada mountain ranges run along the entire Pacific Coast and act as a barrier to the humid winds that sweep in off the ocean. These winds leave their moisture in the form of rain on the western slopes of the mountains, where in some areas more than 70 inches of rain falls every year. As a result, when the air reaches the land east of the mountains, it has shed its moisture and become a hot, dry wind. These winds that come from the mountains

The location of deserts in America

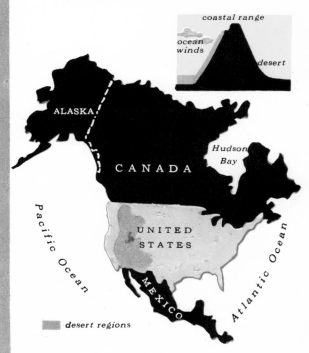

desert regions

help to explain the large desert areas that exist in the United States and Mexico. In some regions little rain falls. And even when rain does come, there are few plants growing to prevent water from running off the land and being lost.

The large deposits of lava in the Columbia Plateau are in some places thousands of feet deep.

The Columbia Plateau

The Mojave Desert

A view of the Grand Canyon in Arizona

Another cause of deserts is the pattern of movement of the atmosphere about the earth. In the regions 15 to 30 degrees north and south of the equator dry air from high altitudes sinks to the surface. As this air sinks, it is warmed and it becomes even drier. This movement of air causes the deserts of the southwestern United States, as well as those in North Africa, Arabia, Iran, West Pakistan, South Africa, and Australia.

THE DESERTS OF AMERICA

Much of the Columbia Plateau was formed by volcanic action many millions of years ago. Lava at one time poured out of vast cracks in the earth and covered the land. In some places this lava is several thousand feet deep. With adequate water, the lava beds that remain provide very good soil for growing crops.

South of the Columbia River Plateau is the Great Basin, a region of over 200,000 square miles that lies between the western wall of the Rockies and the eastern wall of the Sierra Nevada. It includes land in Oregon, Idaho, Nevada, Utah, and California. The Great Basin is rocky desert, eroded by winds and divided into valleys by rugged mountain ranges. The Basin gets little rain, and none of the rivers and streams in the area find their way to the sea. They simply disappear into the ground from temporary lakes known as playas. In ancient times, much of the Great Basin was covered by large salt lakes. The largest of these was Lake Bonneville. It was once 1,000 feet deep. Today only a small part of the area that was once Lake Bonneville contains any water at all. That area is the Great Salt Lake, which is only about 12 feet deep. The rest of the area is now long, flat expanses of dry land. These flats are used as tracks where automobile speed trials are run.

One of the most famous deserts in the Great Basin is Death Valley. This region of nearly 2,000,000 acres is so remarkable that it was made a national monument in 1933. The lowest point in the valley, called Badwater, is 280 feet below sea level. In summer, the temperatures in Death Valley rival those of the Sahara, climbing as high as 134 degrees Fahr-

enheit. The only water found is in salt pools. Death Valley got its name in 1849 when a group of gold miners attempted to cross the valley as a short cut and became lost.

Another desolate region—the Mojave Desert—lies south of Death Valley. It is a 15,000 square mile region of dry lakes, desert valleys, and barren mountains that rests on a lava base. The Mojave Desert, like Death Valley, contains some gold, as well as valuable deposits of borax.

Arizona also contains many desert regions. The best known is the Grand Canyon. This vast gorge, over 200 miles long and about a mile deep, has been cut into the layers of rock of the Colorado Plateau by the Colorado River. The Grand Canyon is four miles wide at its narrowest point and as wide as 18 miles in some places.

LIFE IN THE DESERT

Animals and plants manage to live in the deserts in spite of the harsh conditions. Plants grow in all but the most extreme desert areas. Such plants are especially adapted to desert life. Their leaves lose little moisture. Their stems often store water and their water-seeking roots dig deep into the earth. Individual plants are spaced far apart. Cactus, mesquite, yucca, and greasewood are some desert plants.

The animals that live in deserts are also adapted to their hot, dry life. One of the most frightening animals is the Gila monster, a poisonous lizard that is about 18 inches long. Its skin is covered with scales, and thus little water is lost through the pores. The Gila monster stores food in its large tail. Mice, rabbits, coyotes, and even some kinds of deer manage to live in deserts. Snakes, scorpions, and tortoises also survive, as do some types of owl, sparrow, and hawk. The number of animals is not large, but there are always some animals living in deserts.

Man also can live in the desert. In some regions, such as the Imperial Valley in California, which used to be part of the Colorado

A few places in deserts in the United States have been irrigated and are used for farming, but most of the desert area is uninhabited.

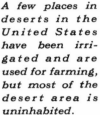

(Above) The Great Basin
(Left) In many parts of the desert the most practical means of transport is a jeep.

River delta, irrigation has been successfully. Water from the Colorado River has made it possible to grow crops, such as melons, alfalfa, and grapefruit. As more and more dams and canals are built, man will be able to use more of the desert areas for farming.

At the present time, however, some of the unirrigated desert regions are used for testing weapons. The first atomic bomb was exploded in a desert in New Mexico. The White Sands Proving Grounds, also in New Mexico, has been an important site for testing rockets. And such experimental craft as the rocket-powered X-15 use the vast salt plains of Muroc Lake in California as a landing field when they return from test flights.

Japan—Land of the Rising Sun

The nation of Japan is made up of a chain of mountainous islands located in the Pacific Ocean, east of China. Some 600 of Japan's islands are inhabited but most of Japan's 142,801 square miles are included in the four largest islands. They are Honshu, Shikoku, Kyushu, and Hokkaido. The capital city, Tokyo, is on the island of Honshu.

Japan is only about the size of the state of California, but its population of about 92,000,000 is almost eight times larger than Califor-nia's. What's more, Japan's population is growing at a rate of about 1,000,000 people a year.

Since the islands of Japan are actually the tops of an underwater mountain range, very little of the land is flat. It is made up of high mountains and small valleys more than half-covered with forests. Japan has about 150 volcanoes, and about 40 of these are still active. The most famous volcanoes are Mt. Aso and Mt. Fuji. Aso has the largest crater of any volcano in the world. Fuji is Japan's highest mountain. Because of the mountains and volcanoes there are many earthquakes in Japan. The worst one, in 1923, destroyed most of Tokyo and killed thousands of people.

Most of the land in Japan is too rocky to be good for farming. And most of the land that can be planted is devoted to growing rice. Rice is Japan's most important farm crop. But bar-

The flag of Japan

JAPAN
AREA: *142,801 square miles*
POP: *90,900,000*
CAPITAL: *Tokyo*
RELIGIONS: *Buddhist, Shinto, Christian*
LANGUAGE: *Japanese*
MONETARY UNIT: *Yen (0.2¢)*

The tea ceremony is an ancient and stylized ritual. It is performed by Japanese families that still observe some traditional customs. Since World War II many Japanese families have become westernized, but it is not unusual for them to live traditionally at home. Frequently adults and children change from western clothing into kimonos when they return from school or work.

ley, wheat, and mulberry trees are also grown. The mulberry trees provide food for silkworms. These worms produce a thread which is made into silk in Japanese factories.

Japanese history goes back many centuries. The earliest history of the islands is told in tales and legends. The name Japan has an odd origin. The Chinese name for the country was Jimpen-kuo, which means: the country where the sun rises. Even now, centuries later, Japan is known as the Land of the Rising Sun.

Since the fifth century, Japan has been ruled by emperors. But from the fifth century until the 19th, shoguns—military governors—gradually took over the power of the emperor. In 1868 the office of shogun was abolished and the power of the emperor was restored.

Trade brought an end to Japan's years of isolation.

JAPAN

It was not until the 16th century that people in Europe visited Japan. In 1542, a Portuguese trading ship was wrecked off the Japanese coast. The shipwrecked merchants stayed in Japan. They told other Portuguese settlers in the Far East about this new place to trade. In 1549, the merchants in Japan were joined by another European. A Jesuit missionary, St. Francis Xavier, came to teach Christianity to the Japanese people. Other Jesuit priests followed him.

The Japanese had three chief religions in which they believed strongly. They were Buddhism, Confucianism, and Shintoism. The Jesuit missionaries had a difficult time. However, they did manage to convert many people. The more the people accepted Christianity, the angrier the Buddhist priests became. Only the help of a great Japanese leader, Nobunaga, kept the priests from sending all the missionaries out of Japan. Nobunaga did not believe in Christianity, but he knew the Japanese could learn a great deal from the Europeans.

Finally, in 1638, the European missionaries were forced to leave Japan. The merchants were allowed to stay. But, in 1640, the merchants were told to leave too. Japan remained almost totally cut off from the rest of the world for almost 200 years. No Japanese was allowed to go abroad, and no foreigner could come to Japan. This situation lasted until 1854, when Commodore Matthew Perry brought a message from the President of the United

This drawing is made from a painting of 1794. It is a picture of two Japanese actors who performed in the Kabuki theater of the 18th century.

States to the Japanese. The United States wanted Japan to open for trade. Perry's expedition was successful.

By the end of the 19th century, foreigners were free to come and go. They even started industries in Japan. Specialists from many places taught the Japanese modern methods. Japan changed very rapidly from a simple agricultural country to an industrial nation. Telegraphs and railroads tied together the parts of the empire which had been separated for centuries by mountains and seas. Manufacturing was added to fishing and farming as a way to earn a living. And over the years Japan built a large navy.

It was partly because of this navy that

The traditional Japanese hair styles are worn today mostly by older women and for special ceremonial occasions such as weddings. The hair is elaborately dressed and held with many pins and combs.

COMBS

Japan won so many victories during World War II. For some time after her attack on the United States naval base at Pearl Harbor, Japan fought successfully against the Western allies. But little by little she neared defeat by the Allied powers. Finally, when the United States dropped atomic bombs on the Japanese cities of Hiroshima and Nagasaki, Japan surrendered.

After the surrender a democratic form of government was developed for Japan. And Japan became Westernized in other ways, too. Japanese cities look more and more like those in the United States and Europe. Japanese men and women usually wear western-style clothing. Some women still wear the traditional kimono, and some men wear western clothing during the day and change to kimonos when they get home from work. When Japanese people return home from their activities, they remove their shoes before entering the house. Everyone must remove his shoes before entering a Japanese home. This is done in order to keep the straw floor mats from getting dirty.

Japanese houses are small and simple. The rooms are not separated by doors. Instead, they are divided with sliding partitions called shoji. Shoji are panels of thin rice paper or glass framed with wood. There is very little furniture in the rooms. Sometimes there is only a very low dining table. For sleeping and sitting, the Japanese use pillows placed right on the floor mats. Decoration is often limited to beautiful flower arrangements. And many Japanese

On one of the Japanese islands there lives a group of people known as the Ainu. They are very different racially from the other Japanese. It is thought that they migrated to the Japanese Islands sometime during the prehistoric ages.

Japanese farm women work in the neatly planted gardens and fields along with the men.

SHOES

women go to schools to learn the art of arranging flowers. Almost every home has a small garden designed with great care, with a special place for each plant and rock.

Although the Japanese people love the traditions and culture of their past, they have been quick to accept the modern ways of the West. Their factories produce cloth, machinery, chemicals, china, and paper. These products are shipped all over the world. Japan is also the world's greatest supplier of fish. From a country that was, for many centuries, cut off from the rest of the world, Japan has become an important center of trade and industry.

An iceberg may be very large. This ice mountain, seen in 1940, was 1,846 feet long, 331 feet high above the surface of the water, and about 1,700 feet deep below the water.

Icebergs

Icebergs are floating islands of ice, broken off the icecap of Greenland and the Antarctic continent by the action of waves and tides and by the slow movement of glaciers into the sea.

Many thousand icebergs are formed every year. More than half of these come from the 5,500,000 square mile ice-covered continent of Antarctica. But the icebergs that come from West Greenland are the most dangerous because they drift down into the North Atlantic shipping lanes and menace passing ships and fishing fleets.

Icebergs vary in size and shape. Those in the Antarctic are usually very large, have steep clifflike sides, and are flat on top. The largest may be 50 or more miles long and over 2,000 feet thick, with walls rising 200 to 300 feet above the sea. The icebergs in the North At-

lantic are much smaller than those in the Antarctic. They are usually irregularly shaped so they look like floating mountain peaks. They are seldom over 800 feet long or 300 feet above the water. In determining the size of an iceberg, it must be remembered that only about one sixth of an iceberg shows above water.

Long arms of ice extend into the sea from the coast of Greenland. The waves and tides beat against these, and with the roar of an explosion large chunks break off to form icebergs. About 7,500 sizable icebergs are detached from West Greenland glaciers each summer.

When icebergs are detached they drift north and west, pushed by the ocean currents —often against the wind—across Baffin Bay and the Davis Strait to the coast of Baffin Island. The Labrador Current then carries them

(*Right*) *The changing tides and the movement of the waves break icebergs from the ice sheet. These icebergs slip into the water and drift.*

(*Below*) *Ice weighs only a little less than water, so most of the iceberg remains hidden beneath the surface. This makes it difficult for ships' captains to judge how close they can approach an iceberg without damaging their ships.*

south at the rate of one or two miles an hour toward Newfoundland, the Grand Banks, and the northern shipping lanes.

Many icebergs are caught in the inlets along the coasts of Newfoundland and Labrador and are melted by the summer sun. Others drift farther south, where they are melted by warmer water and air. Nevertheless, some large icebergs have drifted south of New York. In 1926 the remnant of an iceberg was seen 185 miles south of Bermuda.

For many hundreds of centuries icebergs have melted on Newfoundland's Grand Banks, where the warm waters of the Gulf Stream run north. When an iceberg melts, bits of earth and stones, picked up when the ice was part of a glacier moving over land, drop to the ocean floor. At some points the water of the Grand Banks is only 120 feet deep, partly because of this constantly deposited earth.

Icebergs can be extremely dangerous to shipping. One of the worst accidents in seafaring history took place on the night of April 14, 1912. The ship *Titanic*, on the fifth night of its journey out of Southampton harbor, struck an iceberg located about 425 miles south of Newfoundland. It was the ship's first voyage. She had been hailed as unsinkable and as the finest ship of her day. More than 2,000 people were aboard the *Titanic* when she collided with the iceberg. By the next day, the ship and more than 1,500 of her passengers were buried beneath the sea.

As a result of this tragic accident, all transatlantic ships were ordered to cross the ocean by a more southerly course. The International Ice Patrol was formed in 1914 to protect ships from similar accidents. 14 nations now help to support this patrol, which is operated by the United States Coast Guard. The North Atlantic Ice Patrol, as this branch of the Coast Guard is called, keeps track of icebergs and warns ships of their location. Instruments, such as radar, are used to help locate the icebergs, which are often hidden by fog.

A new weapon has been developed recently to help protect ships from icebergs. This weapon is a weather satellite. Tiros I, the first weather satellite launched by the United States, relayed photographs to earth which showed patches of gray in the St. Lawrence River and Gulf of St. Lawrence. Scientists studied the photographs and guessed that the gray patches might be ice floes. They checked with Canadian weathermen and found that they were correct. This experience has given scientists the hope that in the future icebergs can be accurately tracked by weather satellites.

The development of such equipment as the weather satellite, more powerful ice-breaking ships, and the patrol of sea lanes by the Ice Patrol have lessened the danger of icebergs from the north. And the airplane is making the Antarctic wall of ice a hurdle that can be flown over, rather than the impenetrable barrier to man that it once was.

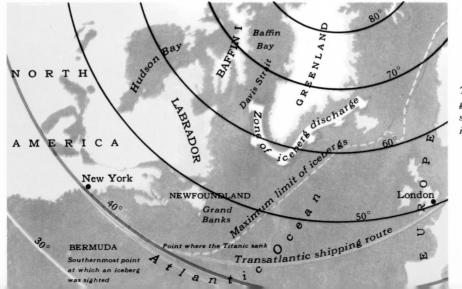

The icebergs most dangerous to transatlantic shipping come from the island of Greenland.

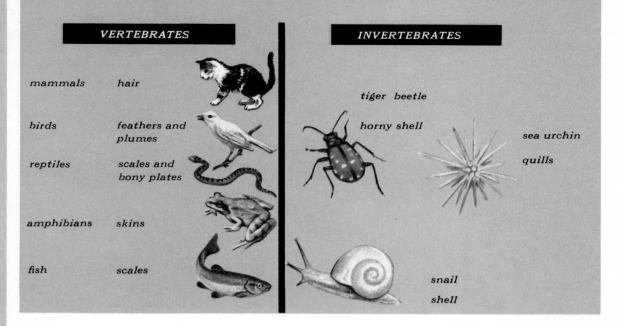

mammals — hair

birds — feathers and plumes

reptiles — scales and bony plates

amphibians — skins

fish — scales

tiger beetle — horny shell

sea urchin — quills

snail shell

How Animals' Bodies Are Protected

In order to survive, all animals must protect themselves and be adapted to their environment. Usually nature helps them by providing them with a body covering that is well suited to the place in which the animals live and to the way they live.

When an animal's body covering is not protection enough against changes in temperature, the animal adjusts by changing its environment. Most birds, for instance, cannot live in very cold places because their feathers will not keep them warm enough. Therefore, they migrate to warmer places during the winter season. Land animals, such as bears, cannot migrate because they cannot travel as far and as fast as birds. Some bears hibernate during the winter. Others grow a heavier covering of fur to protect them from the cold.

The great variety of body coverings that animals have can be seen by studying just one group of animals—the mammals. The bodies of most mammals are covered with various amounts of hair. Some mammals have long, coarse hair, while others have short, fine hair. Still others have so much hair that it is described as fur. The kind of covering a mammal has depends on where it lives.

The feathers of web-footed birds such as ducks, geese, and swans are kept oiled with a fat secreted by a gland near the tail. This makes it possible for the birds to fly as soon as they leave the water. They could not fly if their feathers were wet because they would be too heavy.

goose

duck

swan

HOW ANIMALS' BODIES ARE PROTECTED

Gorillas, orangutans, and other apes have very long hair on their backs, but much less on their chests. This is useful because apes, like all mammals, suckle their young. The hair growing on apes' backs protects them from the violent tropical rainstorms that occur often in the parts of the world, such as Africa, where they live. And the hair that grows so densely on the apes' backs also acts as armor to protect them when they are attacked.

The bodies of apes are covered with a long, thick growth of hair.

gorilla

orangutan

The hair of apes that grows on the fore-arms between the hands and elbows grows upward, instead of downward like other hair. This helps to keep rain water from running down toward the hands. With dry hands apes are able to climb trees without slipping.

Mammals that live in colder climates need the protection of longer and thicker hair. The musk ox, for instance, which is found in the northernmost parts of North America and Greenland, has a very thick, long coat of hair which grows down the sides of its body and covers its hoofs.

The body of the white polar bear (1) is covered with a very dense, woolly fur. This makes it possible for the bear to sleep on ice or snow without feeling the cold.

During the cold season the mountain goat (2) is covered with a white coat that is so thick the goat seems much larger than it actually is. During the warmer times of the year the mountain goat sheds part of this coat.

In temperate climates, where cold seasons alternate with warm seasons, mammals change their coats. Dogs (3), cats (4), horses, donkeys, and oxen have heavier coats in winter than in summer. Lions (5), tigers, and other mammals that live in hot climates have short, light coats the year around.

A special kind of hair covers the body of some kinds of mammals. Hedgehogs (6) and porcupines (7) have body coverings made of sharp, strong hairs called quills to protect them from their enemies. When another animal comes in contact with these quills, they embed themselves into the enemy's skin and produce pin wounds. Most animals quickly learn to respect the spiny fortresses on the porcupine's and hedgehog's backs.

Many other animals have coverings that protect them not only from the climate but from their enemies. The turtle, for example, is well protected from attack by the bony shell which encloses its body and into which its head, feet, and tail may be drawn.

The skin of an animal can also be protection. An elephant, for example, has a thick, tough hide to protect it from the brambles and the insects that live in the tropical jungle.

The armadillo (8) has a different body covering from that of any other animal. Its body is protected by a strong shell made up of bony plates. The plates along the back are arranged in such a way that the armadillo can roll up into a ball in times of danger.

Animals' bodies are also protected by their colors. The white fox of the Arctic regions blends so well with the snow-covered land that it can barely be seen by its enemies. The ermine changes its coat from brown in the summer to white in the winter. Nature has equipped each animal with the proper covering to meet its needs for protection and comfort.

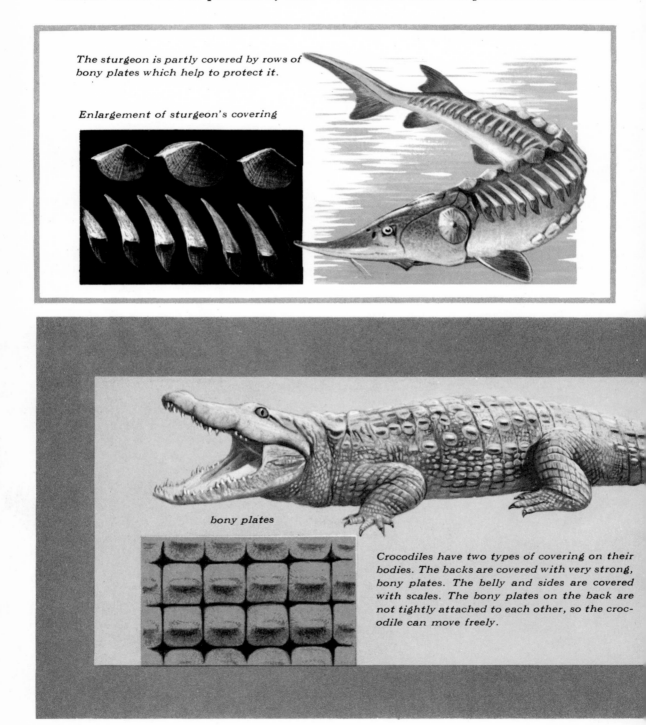

The sturgeon is partly covered by rows of bony plates which help to protect it.

Enlargement of sturgeon's covering

bony plates

Crocodiles have two types of covering on their bodies. The backs are covered with very strong, bony plates. The belly and sides are covered with scales. The bony plates on the back are not tightly attached to each other, so the crocodile can move freely.

Reptiles such as snakes, lizards, and crocodiles are covered with a dry horny or scaly skin. This kind of skin covering retains moisture, which makes it easier for reptiles to live on dry land.

Viper, a common European snake

Enlargement of a piece of snakeskin

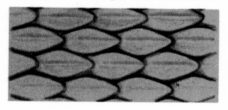

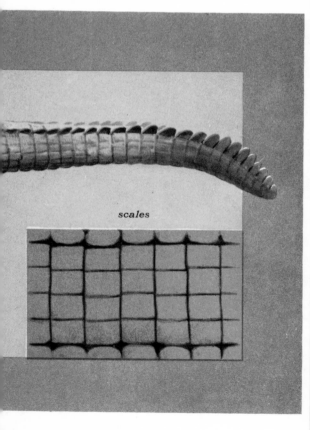

scales

Stone Age Man

Historical records of man's life on earth go back about 5,000 years. But men lived on earth for hundreds of thousands of years before they began to leave a record of their lives. This period is often called the Stone Age because the traces we have found of how these men lived are mostly of stone. They used wood and bone, too, but stone is longer lasting. The term Stone Age does not refer only to prehistory. It is also used to describe a stage of development of peoples. There are some people on earth today, such as the Australian Bushmen, who are still in the stone age of their development.

The prehistory of Western man is divided into three periods. These periods—named for man's growing knowledge of how to use stone—are the Paleolithic Age, the Mesolithic Age, and the Neolithic Age. *Lithos* is the Greek word for stone. *Paleos* means old, *mesos* means middle, and *neos* means new.

Of the three periods of prehistory, the Paleolithic was the longest. It lasted from about 650,000 years ago until about 8000 B.C. In the earliest part of it, the lower Paleolithic period, man used simple tools made by chipping one stone with another. He lived on raw meat because fire had not yet been discovered.

By Neolithic times, which lasted from 6000 to 4000 B.C., prehistoric man had mastered the use of stone so thoroughly that he was able to build stone houses to live in and could hunt for his food with a bow and stone-tipped arrows. He also learned to weave cloth from animal hair and to make pottery. The first villages date from this period and were built of stone.

Prehistoric times were very long. For every minute of man's recorded history, there were about 180 minutes of prehistory. Our knowledge of the way men lived in prehistoric times is incomplete. But archeologists have been able to reconstruct skeletons of early men and women from unearthed pieces of their bones. And their tools, decorations, and clothing have given clues to their way of life.

This family, from the lower Paleolithic period, has just killed a large, deer-like animal by rolling stones on it from a great height. The mother and father are stripping the meat from their kill. One of their sons is chewing on the raw meat. All food is eaten raw because fire is still unknown. One of the older sons has noticed that some of the stones dropped on the animals have broken into sharp splinters. He is trying to chip off more of these useful, sharp bits of rock which can be held in the hand and used as a crude knife.

During the middle Paleolithic period men found shelter from the intense cold in caves. By this time fire has been discovered, and men no longer flee south before the advancing glaciers. Here, in the cave, some men are cooking meat on sticks over the fire, while another pair works on making a second fire at the other side of the cave. The spears leaning against the cave wall have sharp, pointed flint tips that make hunting much easier than it was in lower Paleolithic times. The people have learned to make crude but warm skin clothing and boots.

The people in this picture lived about 20,000 years ago, in the upper Paleolithic period, and are dressed much like Eskimos. They now know how to tan leather, and well-tanned hides are sewn together with thongs, which the woman is cutting from a piece of skin. She sews with bone needles. The clothing is warm and resistant to snow and wind. From antlers the men are making hunting harpoons, such as the ones leaning against the cave wall. One man is chiseling at the bone, while a companion makes him more flint-headed tools for his work.

By 7000 B.C., during the Mesolithic period, the ice age was over, and men had begun to live in small villages. Here, the men of the village are at work producing tools from horns and stones. One man is making a digging implement. Hot pitch extracted from birch bark is used for glue. Boats and oars were invented during this period. The boats are being used to bring raw materials to the workmen in the village. The houses are raised on stilts over the water to protect the inhabitants from attacks by animals. The dog has already become domesticated.

Plant Sensitivity

Plants are sensitive to their surroundings. Changes take place within a plant as a result of changes outside it. Light, temperature, moisture, gravity, and touch may change the way a plant grows.

Botanists still do not know exactly what causes plants to react to outside stimuli. But it is thought that there are certain substances—called hormones—in every plant that affect its growth. Botanists think that hormones make a plant sensitive to its surroundings. Now they are trying to find out how the reactions take place.

The most common reaction of plants is growth toward light. If you keep a plant on the window sill, its stem bends toward the light so the leaves will get as much light as possible. If the plant is turned around, the stem will bend backward, again moving toward the light.

This movement is believed to be caused by a hormone called auxine. Auxine controls plant growth by making individual plant cells grow longer. When auxine is exposed to light, it is either destroyed or made less active. The plant cells which are facing the light will not grow as quickly as those that are in the shade. The faster growing cells force the plant to bend toward the light.

Plants react to the amount of daylight, too. Flowering depends on this. Some plants, like spinach, bloom only when the days are short and the nights are long. Other plants flower when the days are long and the nights are short. These are the plants that flower in the springtime and summer. Lettuce is one such plant. In a greenhouse, artificial light is used to make the day longer, and lettuce and similar flowers and vegetables can be harvested all year long.

Some plants have a waking and sleeping pattern. For example, the morning-glory and daisy open in the daylight and close when it is dark. When these flowers are exposed to artificial light during the night and kept in the dark during the day, they reverse their pattern and

Some plants react to light and darkness by opening up their leaves during the day and folding them closed at night. If they are kept dark by day and in artificial light at night, they will reverse this pattern.

(Below) A plant bends toward the sunlight. There is less growth on the side of the stem that faces the light than there is on the side in the shade.

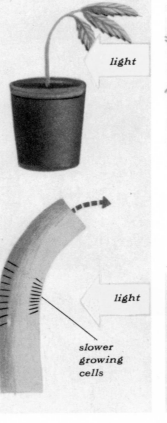

light

light

slower growing cells

Mimosa leaves during the night

Mimosa leaves during the day

Some plants show a waking and sleeping pattern.

Tulips will open if the temperature rises.

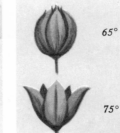

65°

75°

open their blossoms during the night and close them during the day. They are reacting to light and darkness.

Plants are sensitive to changes in temperature, too. A tulip will close if the weather is cool. It will open again when the day becomes warmer. Many other flowers, such as anem-

after leaf closes together quickly. Some of the most dramatic examples of reaction to touch are found among the insect-eating plants, such as Venus's flytrap. If an insect lands on one of its leaves, the leaf will spring shut. The leaf stays closed until the insect has been digested by the plant.

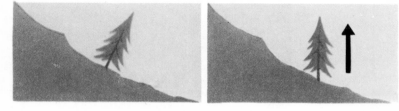

Trees that grow along a hill do not grow at right angles to the slope. They grow straight up toward the sky.

An insect-eating plant catches an insect in a leaf.

A plant's stem grows toward the sky. It will change the direction of its growth to do this.

ones, geraniums, and crocuses, also react to changes in temperature.

Normally, the roots of a plant grow downward. The stem grows upward. If you turn a potted plant on its side, its roots and stems will bend so that they are again growing down and up. Plants react to the pull of gravity, and grow in a vertical direction.

The downward growth of roots may be changed by the presence of water in the ground. Plant roots grow toward water. If the amount of water in the soil is unequal, roots will grow toward the wetter ground. Botanists think that there is a special hormone that makes it possible for roots to find water in the ground and grow toward it.

Grapevines and ivy have long, slender structures called tendrils. Tendrils are sensitive to touch and attach the plant firmly to an object. Tendrils enable vines to grow up around trees and fences. Another plant that is sensitive to touch is mimosa. If you touch one leaf, a wave of movement is set up in the plant. Leaf

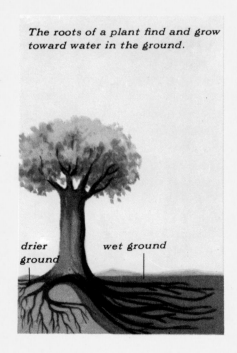

The roots of a plant find and grow toward water in the ground.

drier ground

wet ground

Northern Africa

Five nations form the northern land boundary of Africa, the second largest continent in the world. They are Morocco, Algeria, Tunisia, Libya, and Egypt. These countries stretch in an arc from the Atlantic Ocean in the west, along the Mediterranean Sea, to the Red Sea in the east. All the nations include large parts of the Sahara Desert within their boundaries, except Morocco which is only fringed by the Sahara on the south and southeast.

Central and southern Africa were almost unknown and unexplored by Western man until recent times, but northern Africa's history is long. It is a history of conquest, colonization, and the fight for independence. It is here that the first great western civilization, the Egyptian, flourished. Phoenicians from the eastern end of

Dry river beds are common in the desert where, as the climate became drier, the rivers dried up too.

the Mediterranean Sea built the city of Carthage — near present-day Tunis in Tunisia — in the ninth century B.C. The empire of Alexander the Great included part of this area, and the Egyptian port of Alexandria was built in his honor more than 2,000 years ago. The Romans fought several wars to gain possession of northern Africa, and the ruins of buildings built by the Romans can be seen there today. In the fifth century A.D. Vandals—fierce warriors from central Europe—conquered the Roman colonies. In the seventh century A.D. as the Moslems swept westward from the Arabian peninsula, the lands of northern Africa became part of their empire. The majority of northern Africans are still Arab Moslems.

The Arab invasions were followed by many others—Turkish, French, Spanish, Italian, and British. During the second World War, the strategic importance of these countries was made clear again by the great battles that were fought to gain possession of Tunisia, Libya, and Egypt. Since the war, all the nations of northern Africa except Algeria have become independent.

The nation on the northwest corner of Africa is Morocco. Morocco is isolated from the rest of Africa by the Atlas Mountains, a group of three mountain chains that reach heights of over 13,000 feet. Morocco's longest river—the Oum er Rbia—rises in these mountains.

An Arab warrior. Egypt was under Arabian domination for nearly three centuries, from about A.D. 640 to A.D. 969.

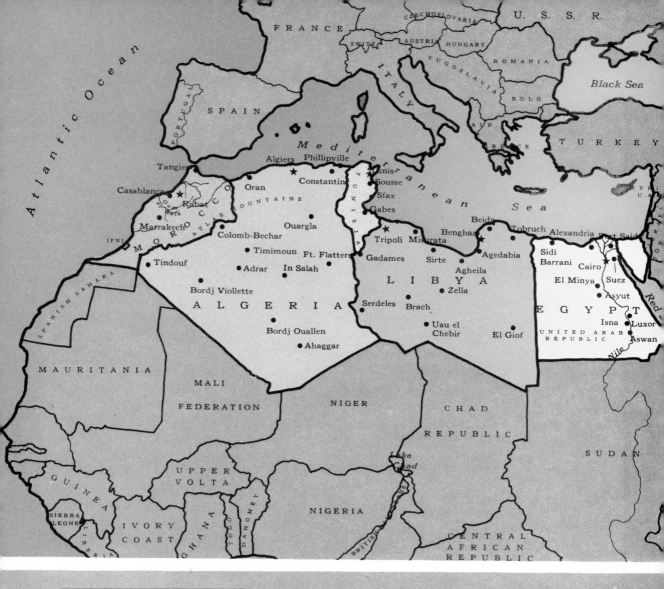

MOROCCO

AREA: *174,553 square miles*
POP: *8,500,000*
CAPITAL: *Rabat*
RELIGIONS: *Moslem, Roman Catholic*
LANGUAGES: *Arabic, French, Spanish*
MONETARY UNIT: *Moroccan franc (.2¢)*

ALGERIA

AREA: *846,124 square miles*
POP: *9,529,700*
CAPITAL: *Algiers*
RELIGIONS: *Moslem, Roman Catholic, Jewish*
LANGUAGES: *Arabic, French*
MONETARY UNIT: *French franc (.2¢)*

TUNISIA

AREA: *48,332 square miles*
POP: *3,800,000*
CAPITAL: *Tunis*
RELIGION: *Moslem*
LANGUAGES: *Arabic, French, Italian*
MONETARY UNIT: *Dinar ($2.38)*

Scale of Miles

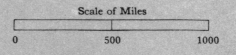

0   500   1000

LIBYA

AREA: *679,358 square miles*
POP: *1,091,830*
CAPITAL: *Tripoli and Benghazi*
RELIGIONS: *Moslem*
LANGUAGES: *Arabic, Italian*
MONETARY UNIT: *Libyan pound ($2.80)*

EGYPT

AREA: *386,198 square miles*
POP: *24,026,000*
CAPITAL: *Cairo*
RELIGIONS: *Moslem*
LANGUAGE: *Arabic*
MONETARY UNIT: *Egyptian pound ($2.87)*

The tomb of the caliphs in Cairo was built in commemoration of the rulers of Egypt who succeeded the Arabians.

The most fertile farms are in the high valleys between the mountain ranges. A variety of crops, including cereals, grapes, figs, and citrus fruits, are grown in Morocco. The chief source of income, however, is minerals, including zinc, lead, manganese, iron ore, cobalt, and phosphates. Morocco is the second largest producer of phosphates in the world.

The two largest cities of Morocco are on the Atlantic Coast. They are Rabat, the capital, and the important port city of Casablanca, one of the fastest growing cities of Africa.

Algeria, Morocco's eastern neighbor, was conquered by France in the period 1830-1909. The French now consider Algeria a part of France. It is approximately four times larger than France.

Almost nine tenths of Algeria, in the area south of the Atlas Mountains, is desert. Oil has been discovered in this otherwise desolate area, and it promises to become a valuable part of the Algerian economy. The northern tenth of Algeria, which lies between the coast and the Atlas Mountains, is a rich farming area. Here the atmosphere and way of life are European. About one third of the farm land is owned by *colons*—European settlers—and the products are similar to those of southern Europe. Wine is the leading export, and citrus fruit, figs, olives, tobacco, grains, and potatoes are also grown. The capital and largest city is Algiers, on the Mediterranean Coast. Algiers is famous for its old quarter, the Casbah, which is crowded with low, old houses and contains many interesting shops and market places. Since 1954 Algeria has been a battleground. The Moslem population wants the country to be free of France. The *colons* do not because they are afraid for their possessions if the Moslems take over the country.

A Moroccan merchant in a typical native costume, called a djellaba

The Atlas Mountains are in southern Morocco.

Rabat, the capital of Morocco

Casablanca, the most important and populous city in Morocco and one of the busiest ports in Africa

Tunisia, a small, independent republic, is located between Algeria and Libya. In Roman times, Tunisia was the leading supplier of grains for the Roman Empire. Today it is able to raise only a little more than enough grains for home use, because land that was once green has gradually dried up, and less than one fourth of the country is now arable. Tunisia's most important exports are iron ore, lead, wines, olive oil, and phosphates. The capital, Tunis, is also Tunisia's leading port on the Mediterranean.

At a well in the Libyan desert, each animal pulls two cords to which a big leather pitcher is attached. When the bucket rises to the surface, the lower cord, which is tied to the bottom of the bucket, is pulled by a man, and the bucket overturns and empties the water into a trough.

Libya is often described as a big box of sand because almost the entire country, which is more than two and one half times the size of Texas, is a riverless desert. Libya has no high mountains, but it is situated on a high plateau that ends abruptly near the coast. One source of income in Libya is stock raising. Nomads raise flocks of sheep near the oases in the desert area called the Fezzan, which is one of the three historical areas into which Libya is divided.

Tripolitania, the northwestern portion of Libya, is the most modern part of the country. Its leading city is Tripoli. The eastern part of Libya is called Cyrenaica, and one of the capitals, Benghazi, is located in this region. A new capital, Beida, is being built in Cyrenaica. Because there is little rainfall, Libyans can farm only in the coastal regions. Oil has been discovered recently in Cyrenaica, and it may provide an important addition to the economy of the country.

Egypt is the most easterly of the northern African nations. This country, which, along with Syria, makes up the United Arab Republic, is as large as Texas, Oklahoma, and Louisiana together. But Egypt is a desert that is able to support life only because of the water of the Nile River, which flows from south to north

A corner of the wool market in Tripoli

53

Mohammed Ali, who has been called the father of modern Egypt, is shown here during a parade in Cairo. In 1805, he was chosen pasha to reign for the Sultan in Turkey. Mohammed Ali enacted important social reforms and extended Egypt to include the Sudan and Syria.

through the eastern third of the country. Rain is almost unknown in Egypt. A narrow band of land on either side of the river is made arable by irrigation. One of the most important projects in modern Egypt is the development of methods to prevent waste of this precious resource—water. Reservoirs and dams are being built for flood control and water storage.

Egypt is one of the world's leading producers of cotton. Rice is grown for export. Egypt also raises fruits, such as figs, oranges, and grapes.

In recent years Egypt has tried to develop industries, such as textile manufacturing, to help support its rapidly growing population. The leading cities are the port city of Alexandria, on the Mediterranean, and Cairo, the capital. Cairo is the largest city in Africa, and the largest in the Moslem world.

Because of its strategic location at the eastern end of the Mediterranean, Egypt has often been a battleground and a colony. The opening of the Suez Canal in 1869 added to Egypt's

Zaghlul Pasha (1860-1927), an Egyptian statesman, was the leader of the Wafd, the first nationalist movement in Africa. His goal was independence.

Fuad I was the first king of Egypt after England gave the nation partial independence in 1922. In 1936, England granted Egypt nearly total independence.

In 1952, General Naguib led a revolution which overthrew the monarchy and established the republic of Egypt. He was succeeded by Gamal Abdul Nasser.

strategic importance, because the waterway is a vital link betwen Europe and Asia. The canal cuts through Egyptian territory from Port Said on the Mediterranean Sea to Suez on the Red Sea. Today the canal is used by about 18,000 ships a year and is an important source of income to the Egyptian government.

Mohammed Idris El Senussi became Libya's first king when that country gained its independence in 1951.

In Tripoli, the Arch of Marcus Aurelius was built by the Romans.

Insect Bites and Stings

Millions of different kinds of insects live on earth, and some of these are natural enemies of mankind. They attack man with bites to obtain food and with stings in self-defense.

A stinging insect has a small, pointed organ at the rear tip of its body. This organ, called a sting, is connected to glands containing a poisonous substance. As it stings, the insect injects some of the poisonous fluid into the wound. These fluids are the substances that make insect stings painful.

Only female insects have stings. In addition to being a weapon of self-defense the sting is the organ through which the female lays eggs.

Some stinging insects have barbs on their stings, like the barbs on fishhooks and arrowheads. These barbs catch in the victim's flesh, and often the sting is pulled out of the insect's body. When this happens, the insect dies. The most common stinging insects of this type are the bee and the wasp.

INSECTS THAT STING OR BITE

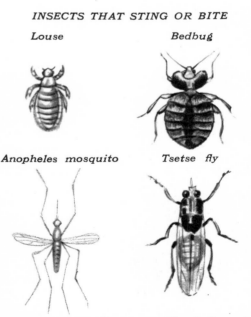

Louse   Bedbug

Anopheles mosquito   Tsetse fly

Biting insects bite to get blood. Some have pointed beaks for piercing the skin and sucking blood. Others have sharp, pincer-shaped jaws and separate blood-sucking tubes. When

1113

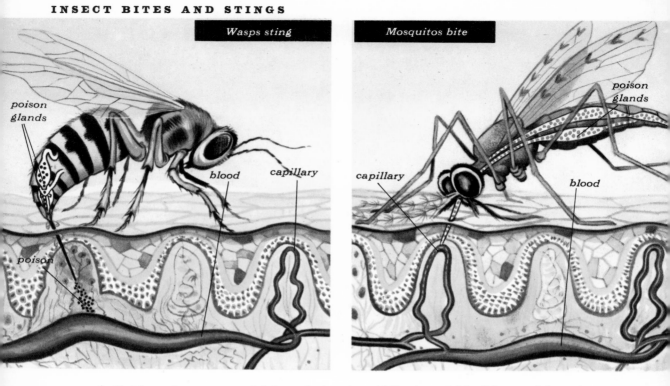

Wasps sting

Mosquitos bite

A sting is used as a means of defense, but an insect bites to suck blood for nourishment.

a mosquito plunges its beak into the flesh of a man or some other warm-blooded animal, it injects into the wound another substance that prevents the blood from clotting. The mosquito is able to do all these things in a fraction of a second. Then it sucks the blood up through its beak as we suck through a straw.

Most insect bites or stings cause discomfort and even pain, but are not really dangerous. It takes more than 500 bee stings, for example, before the poison from a bee is really dangerous to a healthy person who is not allergic to bee venom.

Since the sting often remains in the skin, the first step in treating an insect sting is to take out the sting itself with tweezers or a sterilized needle. To relieve the pain of an insect sting or bite, it is necessary to neutralize the poison. Since insect poisons are always chemically acid, they can be neutralized by a mild alkaline substance, such as a paste of baking soda and water. Some people have very strong reactions to insect stings because they are allergic to the venom. Doctors usually suggest that they take antihistamines by mouth be-

cause the reaction is a general one, not confined to the area of the sting.

Some stings and bites are dangerous because the insect may carry disease germs. If an insect bites or stings a person suffering from certain infectious diseases, it can transmit the disease to its next victim. For example, the anopheles mosquito, which is common in swampy tropical country, transmits malaria. The tsetse fly, of equatorial Africa, transmits sleeping sickness. Body lice transmit typhus, and ticks, which are arachnids, not insects, transmit Rocky Mountain spotted fever.

After years of fighting these insect-carried diseases, man is beginning to win his battle against them. By destroying the places where the insects breed, and by teaching people how to avoid bites, the frequency of the diseases has been brought down. Epidemics are now rare where insect-control is practiced.

But this is a battle that can never end. Insects reproduce with such speed and in such vast numbers that epidemics would soon be back if we ever gave up our fight against the insects that carry disease.

Animals of the Tropical Forest

Tropical forests are made up of three main layers—the floor, the canopy of leaves above it, and the highest tree tops. On the forest floor there is little undergrowth, for the almost solid canopy of leaves over it keeps out most of the light. The atmosphere is always steamy and hot.

The animals that live on the floor spend the middle part of the day in hiding. There is deep silence everywhere. At dawn and dusk the animals come out and move among the shadows hunting for food. The oldest forest animals are the reptiles. There are dozens of kinds of lizards, and turtles, tortoises (1) and toads (2). Snakes such as the anaconda and the boa constrictor (3) are some of the biggest in the world. The bushmaster and the fer-de-lance are two of the deadliest poisonous snakes. Mammals are the most recent animals of the tropical forests. Most of them are small. The largest are the gentle tapir and the jaguar, one of its few enemies.

In the solid canopy of leaves far above the forest floor there are more kinds of tree-dwelling animals than in any other kind of forest. Most of them are acrobats. The monkeys of South America are the only monkeys that can hang by their tails, and there are other animals, too, with prehensile tails. A kind of porcupine, two relatives of the anteater, and several cousins of the raccoon all use their tails to swing through the trees.

Some animals move more sedately among the branches, for they have come up to the canopy to hunt the tree-dwellers. But spider monkeys soar 50 feet from branch to branch, and even reptiles such as a tiny flying lizard leap to branches far above their heads and cling to the undersides with adhesive feet. Others dive into ponds as much as 80 feet below to catch fish. Small snakes sway on the tips of small twigs, while larger ones coil themselves about the tree trunks and wait for their prey to come to them.

Brilliant birds—the parrots, parakeets, macaws, woodpeckers, toucans, hummingbirds, and giant orioles — keep to the canopy layer. They rarely descend to the floor and they almost never fly above the canopy because of the birds of prey waiting above. Most of the canopy animals are meat eaters at least part of the time. The only vegetarians are the squirrel, the porcupine, and the lazy sloth, which spends its life hanging from branches by its claws, inching slowly along in search of leaves to eat.

In the highest layer of the forest—the tree tops that reach over the forest roof—there are few animals during the day. They stay in the canopy to avoid the hawks, eagles, falcons, and owls which are a constant danger. But at dawn and dusk some of the animals come up to gather nuts and fruits. The loudest animals in the world are here—the howler monkeys. They are seldom seen, but their piercing, blood-chilling cries can be heard for miles. They are so loud that one or two monkeys sound like a chorus of dozens.

In every forest layer, from under the earth of the floor to the lofty tops of the tallest trees, are the insects and spiders—gorgeous butterflies, huge caterpillars, and stinging and biting insects—more numerous than anywhere else in the world.

Many tropical birds are beautifully colored. Above are two parrots of South America (4), a lesser bird of paradise of New Guinea and Australia (5), and a tiny hummingbird of Central America (6). The king vulture of South America (7) glides on air currents looking for dead animals, and it can see a mouse on the ground from 5,000 feet up. Among the millions of insects of the tropics are the aedes mosquito (8), the tse-tse fly of Africa (9), and the red ant (10).

Below, left, is the Malayan tapir of southern Asia (11), which has striped offspring (12). The South American iguana (13) climbs trees and dives from great heights. The giant anteater of South America (14) tears ant hills apart with its claws and sweeps up the ants with its sticky foot-long tongue. The fer-de-lance of South America (15) is one of the most poisonous of all snakes. The armadillo of South and Central America (16) rolls itself into an armored ball

when it is attacked. The tarantula (17) is a furry spider with a seven-inch leg spread. Its bite is painful but not poisonous. The Indian python of Asia (18) may grow to be more than 30 feet long. The vicious tayra of South America (19) is a large weasel-like animal that gallops along branches when it hunts.

The South American jaguar (20), above, hunts in the trees and on the ground. The coendou of Central and South America (21), a tree-dwelling porcupine, has a grasping tail. The spider monkey (22) and the howler monkey (23) both live in South America. The three-toed sloth of South America (24) is the most sluggish of animals. The little flying dragon (25) is from southeast Asia and Indonesia. It really glides from tree to tree, rather than flying.

(The animals pictured here are not drawn to scale, and they would never be found all together since they live on different continents.)

Germany

The history of Germany has seldom been the history of one nation. Until 1871 Germany was a group of states rather loosely tied together along with other countries under the Holy Roman Empire. In 1871 Germany became a unified kingdom for the first time. After World War II, however, Germany was again divided, this time into two separately governed sections, West Germany and East Germany.

The geographical boundaries of Germany have changed constantly, too. Germany is located in the middle of the European continent, with no natural barriers to separate it physically from other countries. Its boundaries have expanded and contracted repeatedly. To the north, Germany reaches to the Baltic and North Seas, and it is presently bordered by nine different countries. During the centuries, it has been in direct contact with almost every country in Europe. Germany is a heavily wooded country, in which great forests, such as the Black Forest with its massive dark fir trees, have been carefully preserved. There are many large rivers which provide transportation and hydroelectric power.

The first Germans are believed to have migrated from South Russia. At the time of the Roman Empire, they were described by a Roman historian as rough barbarians, tall, fair-skinned, and blue-eyed, wearing furs and hides.

Various German barbarian tribes conquered and settled England, North Africa, and most of Europe after the decline of the Roman Empire.

When the Roman Empire began to crumble, the German tribes poured into southern Europe, conquering and destroying wherever they went. The German tribes called Goths went down into Italy and Spain. The Vandals went as far as North Africa, across the Mediterranean. The Angles and Saxons went into England. The Franks went into France and built a strong kingdom there. This kingdom, under a series of Frankish kings, became the most powerful of all the German empires.

The greatest of the Franks was Charlemagne, who became king in A.D. 768. Under his rule the Germans controlled Germany,

Martin Luther was a religious reformer who attacked the authority of the Catholic Church. His teachings began the Protestant Reformation.

France, and northern Italy. In 800, as a reward for forcibly converting the Saxons to Christianity, the Pope in Rome made Charlemagne emperor of what was called the Holy Roman Empire.

After the death of Charlemagne this Empire collapsed. In the Treaty of Verdun, which was signed in 843, Charlemagne's empire was divided into three separate states. Germany itself became a series of duchies, loosely held together by a German king.

The areas of the different Germanic tribes in the fifth century B.C.

In 1356 Charles IV, a Hapsburg emperor from Austria, wrote what was known as the Golden Bull. This document named electors from seven German districts who had the right to elect the future Holy Roman Emperors. The electors were occasionally more powerful than the emperor himself. For example, Charles V, the emperor who also ruled Austria, Spain, the Netherlands, Naples, and Sicily, was unable to prevent Martin Luther from preaching Protestantism because some of the electors supported him.

Many Germans were converted to Luther's new Protestantism. The local princes, or electors, finally reached an agreement that each state could decide upon its own form of religion. But in 1618. a great religious war broke out, known as the Thirty Years War. Many countries fought on each side in this war, but most of the battles took place in Germany. By the terms of the treaty that ended the war, the Holy Roman Empire and its Hapsburg emper-

One of the famous leaders of 18th century Prussia was Frederick II, called Frederick the Great.

ors lost most of their power. It was the German people, however, who were hardest hit. It is estimated that one third of the population was killed or died of starvation during the war.

In the 18th century a new power—the kingdom of Prussia—arose in northern Germany. The Hohenzollern family, who ruled the country, built up Prussia as a great military power. The most famous member of the family was Frederick II, known as Frederick the Great. He was a highly educated man who encouraged the writers, artists, and musicians who flourished in 18th century Germany. At the same time, he believed in military might. Because Prussia was a low plains country and had no natural defense against invasion, he built up a large army. Later, when the Prussians were defeated by Napoleon during the Napoleonic wars, the state added the first compulsory military service for all citizens.

After Napoleon's defeat the Congress of Vienna, in 1814 and 1815, grouped 39 German states, including Austria, into a German Confederation, with an assembly but no ruler. In the following years there was a great strug-

Count Otto von Bismarck made Prussia strong.

gle for leadership of the new Confederation between the Hapsburgs of Austria and the Hohenzollerns of Prussia.

This struggle continued until the Prussian King Wilhelm I came to the throne. Wilhelm had as a minister an extremely skillful statesman, Prince Otto von Bismarck-Schönhausen. It was Bismarck who finally brought the Hohenzollerns to power. He instigated a war with Austria in 1866, which the Prussians won. Then he was able to organize a new North German Confederation that left out Austria. A few years later Bismarck maneuvered France into declaring war on the German states and defeated her. France was forced to give Germany the border state of Alsace and part of Lorraine. After this Prussian victory, all the southern German states joined the Confederation, and in January, 1871, a new German empire—the first unified Germany—was formed with the king of Prussia as its Kaiser

Under Bismarck's guidance the new German empire prospered. German industries were developed, and colonies in Africa and in the Pacific islands were added to its territories.

In 1871 the German Empire was formed under the Prussian King.

After Prussia defeated France in 1870, Bismarck received the surrender of Napoleon III.

In 1888, however, a new Kaiser, Wilhelm II, came to the throne, and in 1890 he forced Bismarck to resign. He directed his new ministers to build up a great army and navy, and the country became so heavily armed and militaristic that France, Russia, and Great Britain formed a mutual protection alliance known as the Triple Entente. By 1914 Germany was involved in World War I, and by 1917 the United States had joined the Allies fighting against Germany. Germany was defeated in 1918, and Kaiser Wilhelm left the country to take refuge in Holland.

In the peace treaty at Versailles that followed, Germany lost its colonies and part of its European empire. It had to pay a large sum in reparations for the damage it had done.

After the war Germany became a republic, known as the Weimar Republic. Its government was democratic with an elected assembly, a president, and a chancellor. But the Weimar Republic was opposed by many factions within the country, and discontent and despair became widespread when Germany suffered a terrible inflation in the value of its money, followed by a great depression.

In 1920 a small group of men who called themselves National Socialists, or Nazis, began to attract attention among the German people. The Nazis were led by Adolf Hitler, who attacked the government, the socialists, and the Jews. In 1923 Hitler and others tried to seize the government. This attempt, which was called the Beer Hall *Putsch,* failed and Hitler was jailed. While in jail, he wrote a book called *Mein Kampf,* which expressed his ideas. Many Germans who were out of work and hungry listened eagerly to this new leader who promised them power and prosperity.

By the end of 1932 the Nazi party had 197 seats in the Reichstag, the German assembly. In 1933 Germany's president, Field Marshal von Hindenburg, recognized the Nazis' power by making Hitler chancellor. When von Hindenburg died in 1934, Hitler made himself both president and chancellor, under the title *fuehrer,* or leader.

The Reichstag, controlled by Hitler's National Socialist party, voted him dictatorial powers. Hitler set up People's Courts and appointed judges who convicted any person who opposed him. He built concentration camps for political prisoners. He wrote the Nuremberg laws which deprived Jews of virtually all rights. Thousands of Jews fled Germany. Hitler and his followers set out deliberately to exterminate all that remained. It is estimated that more than 6,000,000 Jews were murdered before Hitler was finally defeated. Because churches opposed the Nazis, a great many

The main industrial cities in modern Germany

WEST GERMANY
AREA: *95,918 square miles*
POP: *54,373,000*
CAPITAL: *Bonn*
RELIGIONS: *Protestant, Roman Catholic, Jewish*
LANGUAGE: *German*
MONETARY UNIT: *Deutsche mark (23.81¢)*

EAST GERMANY
AREA: *41,645 square miles*
POP: *17,832,200*
CAPITAL: *East Berlin*
RELIGIONS: *Protestant, Roman Catholic, Jewish*
LANGUAGE: *German*
MONETARY UNIT: *Deutsche mark (East) (no established rate of exchange)*

ministers and priests were also persecuted.

Hitler was determined to expand the boundaries of Germany, which he called the Third Reich. Germany withdrew from the League of Nations in 1933. In 1938 Germany annexed Austria and, after an agreement with Britain and France, took the Sudetenland portion of Czechoslovakia. In 1939 it seized the rest of Czechoslovakia. Germany made a non-aggression pact with the Soviet Union in 1939.

On September 1, 1939, Germany invaded Poland. Two days later Great Britain and France declared war on Germany. Later Germany attacked the Soviet Union, and it joined the Allied side. The United States, after being attacked by Germany's ally Japan, joined the Allies in 1941.

Germany's defeat came in 1945. The Western Allies drove into Germany from the west and the Soviet Union pressed forward from the east. On April 30, 1945, as the Allies were entering Berlin, Hitler committed suicide. A week later Germany surrendered unconditionally.

After the war Germany was divided into four zones under the military governments of France, Great Britain, the United States, and the Soviet Union. The city of Berlin was also divided into four zones governed by the four powers. In 1948 the three Western powers united their zones in Germany into a common state—West Germany—and authorized the West Germans to form a government. The Soviet Union withdrew from the alliance, making their occupation zone a separate state— East Germany.

The West German Federal Republic was formed in 1949, and it was given complete independence in 1955. The West German capital is in Bonn. The government is a representative one with candidates elected by secret ballot. A president heads the Republic and nominates the chancellor, who is elected by a majority vote of the parliament.

The East German state, with its capital in East Berlin, was proclaimed independent by the Soviet Union in 1954. Believing that the Soviet Union still really controlled the country, however, the Western powers refused to recognize East Germany as an independent state.

Jet and Rocket Engines

The jet engine is recent, but knowledge of the principles behind it is old. The Greeks knew that steam rushing out of a closed kettle exerted a force on the kettle walls. Sir Isaac Newton, the 17th century English physicist, clearly explained the forces of reaction that make a jet engine work. His third law of motion states that "for every action there is a reaction equal in force and opposite in direction." This means that when a powerful stream of water rushes out of a fire hose, the force—action—of the water rushing forward pushes back on the nozzle with equal force—reaction.

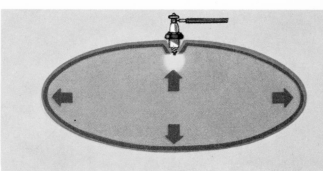

A jet engine depends upon the same principle. When a mixture of fuel and air inside a sealed container is ignited by a spark, there is a violent expansion of hot gases. These gases push in every direction against the walls of the container—action—but the walls resist with equal force—reaction. No gases are able to escape, and the container remains immobile.

If, however, a hole is made at one end of the container, the expanding gases will rush out of this hole. As a result, there will be no pressure on the wall at this point. At the other

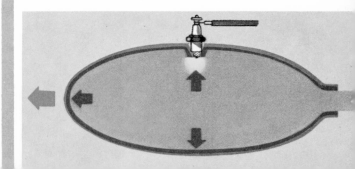

end of the container, however, the gases still exert a pressure outward. This now unbalanced force moves the container forward, in the direction opposite to that of the escaping gases. This principle of action and reaction is utilized in jet engines and rocket engines, both of which depend upon the ejection of a stream of gases.

THE RAM-JET

The simplest jet engine is the ram-jet, nicknamed the flying stovepipe. Simple though this engine is, it was not until 1945 that an American ram-jet made its first flight. A ram-jet is simply a tube open at both ends, with no moving parts. As the plane moves through the sky, air is scooped into the front of the tube by the high speed. It is then mixed with fuel and ignited. The air and gases cannot move out of the front because more air is constantly being rammed into the front of the tube. The reaction, as the gases are ejected at the rear, pushes the plane forward.

The ram-jet is very powerful, but it has one handicap. The tube must be moving through the air at more than 200 miles per hour before the ram-jet will start to work. At less than 200 miles per hour, the air does not enter the tube fast enough for the ram-jet effect to work. For this reason, planes or missiles that use ram-jet engines have to be launched with some type of booster before the ram-jet can be turned on.

THE TURBOJET

The turbojet is the most widely used type of jet engine. Unlike the ram-jet, the turbojet can be started with the plane standing still on the ground. It does not need a high-speed push from a booster. A turbojet is really a ram-jet with moving parts.

The turbojet has three essential parts—the compressor, the combustion chamber, and the turbine. The compressor, which is like a many-bladed fan, sucks air into the front of the engine and compresses it. The air, which is heated by being compressed, next passes into the combustion chamber where the fuel—usually a cheap gasoline or kerosene—is injected into the air stream and ignited. The ignition is

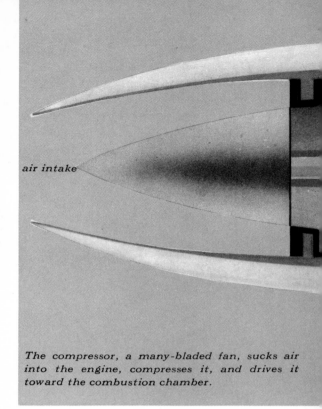

air intake

The compressor, a many-bladed fan, sucks air into the engine, compresses it, and drives it toward the combustion chamber.

continuous, so that constant explosion and expansion is taking place.

The expanding gases rush out of the combustion chamber through the fanlike blades of the turbine. The rapid passage of the hot gases causes the turbine to rotate at a very high speed. It may reach as many as 16,000 revolutions per minute. The turbine and compressor are connected. It is the turbine in the rear of the turbojet that turns the compressor in front Once the engine is started, the jet of gas at the rear thrusts the airplane ahead and, by turning the turbine, operates the compressor and brings in a continuous supply of fresh air.

The gases leaving the turbines may rush out of the engine at speeds of 1,200 miles per hour. The speed of the plane, however, depends not only on the speed of the exhaust gases, but also upon their mass. Some jet engines take advantage of this by injecting a mixture of water and alcohol into the combustion chamber. Water injection adds to the mass of the exhaust gases and can give an engine up to 1,000 pounds of extra thrust. Greater power can also be obtained by adding an after-burner to the engine. This is like adding a second combus-

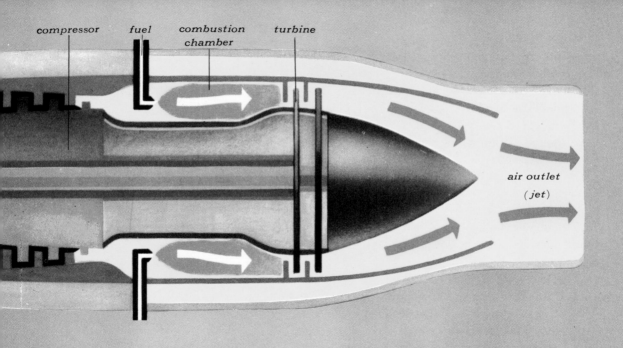

compressor fuel combustion turbine air outlet
chamber (jet)

In the combustion chamber, the air is mixed with fuel. The mixture is ignited, and the expanding gases are forced out through the turbine.

The turbine consists of one or more bladed wheels, which are spun by the hot gas. The turbine, in turn, drives the compressor.

The modern turbojet is an engine that works most efficiently at high altitudes. Some modern engines develop about 20,000 pounds of thrust—almost enough power to drive a navy cruiser.

SOME JET AND ROCKET AIRCRAFT

A turboprop airplane

A ram-jet airplane

A rocket-powered craft

tion chamber after the turbine. The extra fuel burned here gives additional power to the engine.

The turbojet is used to drive big passenger planes, such as the DC-8 and the Boeing 707. A related engine, the turboprop jet, is used on such planes as the Lockheed Electra and Vickers Viscount. The main difference between the two engines is that the turbine in a turboprop jet also drives a propeller in the front of the engine. Turboprops are less powerful than pure jet engines, but they use less fuel.

ROCKET ENGINES

All jet engines need oxygen in order to burn their fuel. As a result, jet engines only work within the earth's atmosphere. The rocket engine—which powers experimental aircraft, such as the X-15, and big rockets, such as the Atlas and Jupiter—has no such limitation. Its chemical fuels provide their own oxygen. The thrust of the rocket explosion drives the Atlas Rocket forward at speeds of about 25,000 miles an hour—more than 30 times the speed of sound. It is rocket engines such as this that will take man into outer space.

Trade has grown from the barter of a few objects of equal value to gigantic commercial enterprises which span the globe. Modern transportation methods make it possible to ship goods safely and quickly over great distances.

Trade and Commerce

When you buy a bottle of milk, or when you buy an automobile, you are engaged in commerce. When the United States buys several thousand tons of coffee from Brazil, the two nations are also engaged in commerce. For commerce is concerned with the buying and selling and the traffic of goods. It is one of mankind's oldest activities.

Commerce first began when men exchanged food or goods among themselves. This kind of commerce, where no money is used, is known as barter. Barter trading still flourishes in many undeveloped parts of the world such as central Africa, but barter is not limited to primitive tribes. When Russia agrees to send oil to Cuba and accepts Cuban sugar in exchange, barter is also involved. In fact, international trade today often takes place on this basis. First, goods are exchanged between countries. Any difference in value is later made up by a shipment of gold.

Among individuals, however, barter is a clumsy form of trade. As a result, certain objects came to be used as a kind of money early in man's history. Among the North American Indians, wampum and beaver skins became common items of barter. In China money at first took the form of small objects, shaped after the goods they were meant to buy. In many other societies, cattle became a common item of barter before primitive forms of money came into existence.

The coining of money by the state itself is thought to have first taken place in Lydia in Asia Minor in about 700 B.C. As money—often in the form of gold and silver—became more common and more reliable, trade and commerce flourished. Commerce was no longer a matter of barter. It had become a matter of buying and selling.

Throughout history, certain nations have engaged in commerce more actively than others. This has been due largely to their geographical positions and the products or raw materials they produced. In ancient times the Egyptians, Sumerians, Phoenicians, and Syrians all carried on a large volume of trade by ship and by caravan. These countries, located on the Nile River, on the trade routes to Arabia, and around the shores of the Mediterranean, were ideally placed for trade with one another. The greatest navigators and traders were probably the Phoenicians, the people who lived along the coast of the country now known as Lebanon. These people traveled to the borders of the known world, carrying the famous cedars of Lebanon, glassware, metal items, and purple-dyed cloth. In the service of the Egyptians, Phoenician sailors voyaged down the western coast of Africa and may have rounded

Barter, the exchange of food or goods, was the first form of commerce used by prehistoric man.

the Cape of Good Hope. It is possible that Phoenician merchants even sailed to England to trade for tin.

With the rise of Greek naval power, however, the Phoenicians' trade dwindled. The commerce of the Mediterranean Sea was handled by Greeks, Romans, and Arabs, and finally by the powerful Italian city states such as Pisa, Amalfi, Genoa, and Venice. During the late Middle Ages, banking houses began to play a vital role in European trade. In Germany and northern Italy banking families such as the Fuggers in Augsburg and the Medici in Florence became important in international trade. The various banks' branches throughout Europe supplied credit for merchants, making it easier for traders to do business. They also spread the practice of keeping exact records and accounts. This helped a merchant know exactly how much money he might have made or lost and made it possible for him to engage in larger and more complex trading ventures.

The discovery of America by Spain in 1492 and the opening of sea routes to India by Portugal in 1497 radically changed world trade. First of all, there was now more money in Europe, brought from the gold and silver mines of Central and South America. More money meant more trade.

There were also new markets in India and the East Indies, and new goods such as silk and

Primitive money often took the form of stone or metal objects.

Coins and bank notes made trade and commercial transactions easier.

spices which, because of the new sea routes, could now be brought more cheaply to Europe.

Finally, the discovery of these sea routes to the Americas and the Far East meant that countries facing the Atlantic Ocean were now in the best location for trade. Portuguese, Spanish, Dutch, French, and British merchant ships ranged over the globe while the commerce of the Mediterranean ports declined.

The commerce of the world was also advanced by many scientific inventions and discoveries that made travel surer and safer. Navigation had often been uncertain, but sailors were now able to employ such navigation instruments as the astrolabe, the mariner's com-

A Roman soldier checks goods carried through a customs post.

The Greeks replaced the Phoenicians as the traders of the Mediterranean area.

pass, and the sextant. Better maps and charts also came into use as the waters of the world were more heavily traveled. Merchants and bankers were now more willing to risk their money in trading ventures since there was less risk that ships and goods would be lost at sea.

In the modern age the development of railways, steamships, airplanes, cable, radio, and telegraph all mean that men can ship goods more safely and more quickly and over greater distances than ever before. Refrigerated ships and railroad cars make it possible for fresh meat raised in New Zealand to be sent to England, halfway round the world, to be eaten. Commerce is carried on among all countries of the world. Some nations—such as those in Africa, South America, or southeast Asia—produce mainly food and raw materials. Others, such as the United States and the European countries, also manufacture finished products.

Today, trade and commerce involve all the steps from the raw material to the consumer.

cotton plant

industry

wholesaler

retailer

consumer

Geography

This carved piece of wood is an Eskimo map of part of a coast. The high and low land is shown, as well as the inlets.

Geography today is a broad science concerned with the study of the earth's surface in all its aspects. In ancient times, however, geography was limited to the study of the shape of the earth and land and to the making of maps.

THE HISTORY OF GEOGRAPHY

The Greeks were the first people to approach geography scientifically. Thales of Miletus, who lived more than 500 years before the birth of Christ, was probably the first man to believe that the earth was round. And Eratosthenes, who lived in Alexandria three centuries later, calculated the size of the earth with considerable accuracy.

The Romans, who were a practical people, relied on geography to help them in the conquest and control of their large empire. Roman geography stressed the location of cities and provinces, and the best trade and military routes.

In the Middle Ages, this practical knowledge of geography was lost to most Europeans. The theories of the Greeks were better known to the Arabs than to the people of Europe. Few people, in fact, were ready to believe Columbus' claim that he could reach Asia by sailing to the west, although the Greeks had shown that the earth was round more than 1,500 years before.

Reconstruction of a map drawn by Eratosthenes

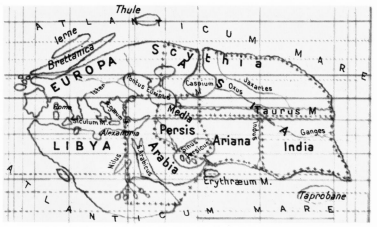

The beginning of modern geography started with the journeys of Marco Polo and the voyages of exploration that finally resulted in the discovery of the Americas. In the year 1522 one of the ships of the Portuguese navigator Ferdinand Magellan returned to Spain after a three year voyage around the globe from east to west. Magellan himself was killed in the Philippine Islands, but he was the man responsible for this remarkable journey. His voyage actually proved for the first time that the earth was a sphere, showed the vast extent of the Pacific Ocean, and revealed that the Americas were not a part of Asia at all.

A 14th century sea chart of Europe shows the earth as flat.

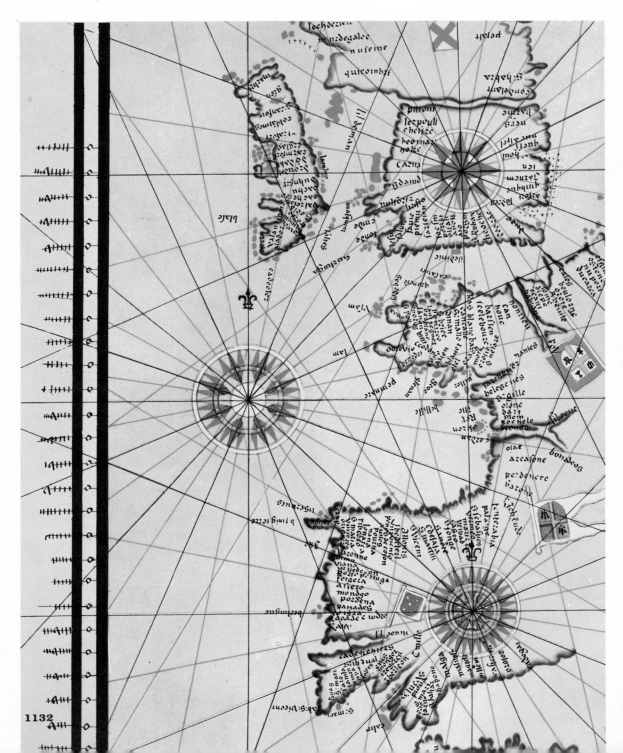

The new discoveries made by such explorers as Columbus, Vasco da Gama, Magellan, John Cabot, Francis Drake, Walter Raleigh, and many others, aroused the interest of scholars as to the true nature of the earth's surface. New plants and animals were brought back to Europe, vast ocean currents were charted, strange native tribes were observed. As man's knowledge of the earth increased, geography was one of the sciences that classified and studied the new items of information.

By the 18th and 19th centuries, reliable maps were in use. The English navigator James Cook had explored the coasts of New Zealand

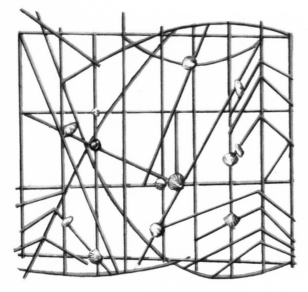

The sailors of some Pacific islands once made maps of interwoven rods. The rods indicated ocean currents and the shells represented islands.

and Australia. In addition, such men as the German traveler Alexander von Humboldt applied scientific principles to the study of geography. He stressed the geographical similarities and differences of parts of the world. Von Humboldt did not limit himself to observing and describing the glaciers of one mountain range. He compared these glaciers with ice formations in other parts of the world, seeking to establish the causes of glaciers and the different effects they produced. Or, in studying climate, he would not simply describe the altitude, position, winds, and rainfall of a certain region. He would also try to determine the ways

in which the climate influenced the human life there.

It is problems such as these that modern geography deals with. Although man has now discovered and explored most of the earth, he

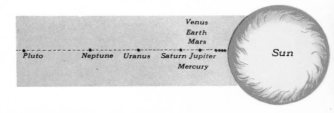

The relationship of the earth to the sun and the other planets

still has many questions to answer about its true nature. The International Geophysical Year—I.G.Y.—which lasted over an 18 month period from 1957 to 1958, was part of a determined effort on the part of scientists from 66 nations to find out more about the earth we live on. New ocean currents were charted. Sheets of ice over 14,000 feet thick were found in the Antarctic. And even man's idea of the shape of the earth was refined. It will take many years before the final results of the I.G.Y. are fully known, but it is ventures like this that advance the progress of geography today.

GEOGRAPHY IN THE MODERN WORLD

Geography today is divided into two parts —regional geography and systemic geography.

The largest telescope in the world is the 200 inch reflector at Mount Palomar in California.

Regional geography concentrates on a certain area of the earth. This area may be small or large. It may be a valley or it may be a continent. Regional geography studies all the aspects of a region and shows the relationships that exist between the varying features in one area. In this way it is possible to study how man, living in one region, has adapted himself to the forces of nature.

Systemic geography studies both physical and human geography. Physical geography studies deserts or mountain ranges or climate

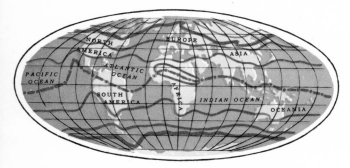

The chart shows the average temperature zones of the earth. The dotted line shows the thermal equator—a line joining all the points that have the highest annual temperature.

as these features occur throughout the world. Human geography is concerned with the relationship between man and geography, showing how the mountains or climate may affect man's way of life. Systemic geography, dealing as it does with the whole surface of the globe, is subdivided into many areas of study. Each of these sciences has been given a name.

Astronomy is concerned with the position of the earth in space, its relation to the sun and the other planets, and the way in which the earth's movement affects such things as the seasons and the length of day and night.

Oceanography studies the oceans, their nature, and their influence upon man. It is a field in which chemists, biologists, physicists, and meteorologists all share their knowledge. Marine biology—the study of the fishes and plants that live in the sea—is a very important branch of oceanography today. It is important because, as the earth becomes more heavily populated, man may one day have to take most of his food from the oceans. The study of the sea bed and the ocean currents is equally important because of its military applications. Nuclear submarines and the threat they pose have caused both American and Russian scientists to probe into the depths of the sea to discover more about what is there. In fact, man knows more about the surface of the moon than he does about the bottom of the oceans.

Climatology studies the climate on various parts of the earth, the effects climate has on man, and records and classifies climates.

Meteorology is concerned specifically with the study of the atmosphere and weather, and big advances are being made in weather forecasting. The launching of space satellites that can record large areas of ocean and cloud is revolutionizing the science of weather forecasting today.

Glaciology studies the formation of glaciers and their great influence on the earth and man.

Geomorphology studies the origin and development of surface landforms, while *geology* is concerned with the structure of the earth's crust, how it has changed over millions of years, and the natural resources buried beneath the earth's surface.

There are many other areas of systemic geography, but all the types of geography listed

(1) *By means of containers that close on command, a ship takes samples of sea water at different depths.* (2) *A ship charts the sea bottom by bouncing sound waves off the ocean bed. The time it takes for the sound waves to return indicates the depth of the sea at that point.* (3) *On the coast, oil that is actually under the sea can be brought up to the surface.*

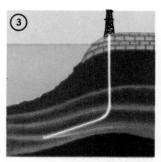

A river has cut a deep gorge through soft rock.

Signposts are stuck into a glacier to measure its rate of flow. Notice that the flow is more rapid towards the center.

above deal primarily with the earth itself and are classed as physical geography.

Human geography is equally important. It studies the distribution of human populations and their relationship with the earth.

Economic geography studies the various activities of man, from agriculture to commerce and industry. This branch of geography relies heavily on figures and statistics to arrive at its conclusions.

Demography is concerned with the size of human populations and why, for example, some countries have higher birth rates than others. The forecasts made by demography can be very useful in revealing what the food needs of the future may be.

Historical geography attempts to describe the geography of mountain ranges during an earlier period, such as the Iron Age, or studies the character of agriculture at the time of the Roman Empire.

Geography, in all its branches, is one of the richest and broadest sciences known to man. In the age of space, when man is exploring the planets, it may seem strange that there is still so much to be learned here on earth. But our future depends in large part upon the way our climate, our natural resources, and human populations are studied—and controlled.

How Fish Breathe

Men breathe with their lungs. The lungs take oxygen from the air into the body and expel the waste product, carbon dioxide, into the air. Fish have gills instead of lungs, but the function of these gills is the same—to inhale oxygen and to exhale carbon dioxide.

The gills are in hollows on each side of the fish's body, directly behind the head. The gill openings have slits in them, which allow water to pass from the fish's mouth, through the gills, and out of the fish's body again.

The gills are made up of layers or threads of very thin membranes that are laced with networks of blood vessels. Oxygen in the water passes through the thin membrane into the fish's bloodstream and carbon dioxide passes through it out of the fish's body.

In bony fishes the gills and the gill openings are covered with tough outer membranes called gill covers. The gill covers open and close rhythmically as the fish breathes. The fish breathes by opening its mouth at regular intervals and drawing in water. The sides of the fish's throat contract, forcing the water back through the gill openings at each side of the throat, over the gills, and out of the fish's body. Valves inside the fish's mouth keep the water from coming back into the mouth.

The water, containing oxygen, circulates through the fish's mouth and out across the gills.

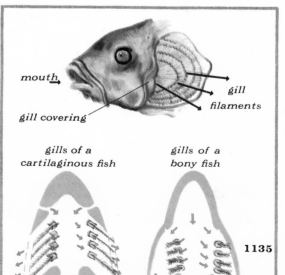

mouth

gill filaments

gill covering

gills of a cartilaginous fish

gills of a bony fish

The exchange of oxygen and carbon dioxide through the membranes during breathing can take place only when the membranes are wet, which is why a fish cannot live long out of water. Without water the gills dry out and the fish dies of asphyxiation.

Scientists believe that the first animal life began in the sea, starting with a one-celled organism. It took in oxygen from the water through the thin walls of its cell. It had to stay in the water, however, because if it got dry it would be unable to breathe and would die.

Gradually, the one-celled creature developed into a more complex organism with many cells. For protection, the many-celled creatures developed tough outer coverings. Then, since individual cells were no longer in direct contact with the water, they could not get their own oxygen. So a breathing system evolved too, and many-celled organisms gradually developed gills.

Eventually some of these water animals ventured onto the land. In order to survive out of water, they had to develop a new way of breathing. Lungs evolved inside the body, where they would not dry out. All the animals that live on land evolved from these first animals that developed lungs hundreds of thousands of years ago.

There are still some kinds of fish today whose development appears to have been stalled in the middle of the evolutionary process from water to land creatures. These fish have lungs and they often have gills, too. They are believed to be of very early origin.

One of these fish, the lungfish, is called a

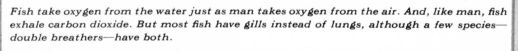

Fish take oxygen from the water just as man takes oxygen from the air. And, like man, fish exhale carbon dioxide. But most fish have gills instead of lungs, although a few species—double breathers—have both.

double breather because it uses both lungs and gills. Its lung is of a primitive type called an air bladder. Lungfish have bony scales, but their skeletons are of cartilage. They have a long, narrow, and leaflike dorsal fin. The lungfish lives in swamps and marshes and breathes air at intervals. In the dry season, when swamps dry out, it sleeps at the bottom of a mud burrow. It leaves a few small holes for air, but the entrance of the burrow is closed by a plug of mud.

Labyrinth fish, which live both in and out of the water, also have lungs in the form of two pouches above the gills. As the dry season approaches, labyrinth fish roam over the land, pushing themselves along with their fins and tails, searching for moist ground. They cannot stay entirely under water for long periods be-

Lungfish

Labyrinth fish

Fighting fish

cause they need air to keep them alive. They also need moisture, however, and in dry seasons they bury themselves in mud.

Another double breather is the fighting fish. This fish is often kept captive by the people of Thailand and used in fighting contests, just as fighting cocks are. The fighting fish has long and tapered fins. When the fish is quiet, its colors are dull. But when it is angry enough to fight, it glows with brilliant color. Fighting fish have lungs as well as gills. Although they never leave the water, these fish frequently rise to the surface to gulp air.

Three of Pizarro's horsemen come upon Cuzco, the capital of the Inca Empire. On the hill is a great fort.

The Incas

In the year 1531 Francisco Pizarro, a Spanish explorer, set sail from Panama with 200 men and 27 horses. His destination was Peru, on the west coast of South America. His purpose was to find and conquer the great empire of the Inca Indians in the same way that Cortes had conquered the Aztecs in Mexico.

This plan of Cuzco shows that the Incas' capital was rectangular in shape and bordered by high walls. The streets were straight and crossed each other at right angles. At the left is the great fort.

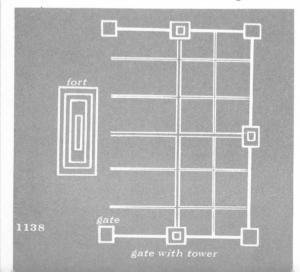

This was a difficult and dangerous task. The borders of the empire were the high mountains of the Andes. And they were defended by thousands of trained soldiers and protected by great forts.

Nevertheless, Pizarro succeeded in making his conquest. He lured the Inca's emperor into his camp, captured and killed him. Then Pizarro invaded the empire. Although the Incas fought bitterly, Pizarro was able to bring them under Spanish control.

This was the end of the enormous, rich empire of the Incas, an empire that had begun hundreds of years earlier.

The first Incas probably came from northern Peru, down to the Cuzco Valley. Here they joined with other Indians, the Quichua, and set out to conquer the neighboring peoples.

The empire grew rapidly. By the time of Pizarro's conquest, the Incas ruled almost 6,000,000 people. Their territory was about 650,000 square miles and covered what is now Peru, Ecuador, Bolivia, and northern Chile.

At the head of all the Incas was the emperor. He ruled his huge land by sending out thousands of officials, each to govern a small part of the country. The emperor held strict control over the people and demanded complete obedience. The people had no possessions except their own houses and household goods. What they grew on their lands belonged by right to the emperor. The people also paid taxes in the form of military service and work for the government.

The emperor lived in the capital city, Cuzco. Even today Cuzco is a beautiful sight. A Spanish explorer in the 16th century wrote:

"The capital of the Incas is a large city located in a broad valley. It is divided into four parts according to the points of the compass. It has about 20,000 inhabitants. The houses and palaces of the nobles are of a splendor and luxury that cannot be imagined. The largest and most impressive building is the fortress of the city. It is constructed of enormous blocks of stone. It is hard to understand how the Indians carried these stones because they have neither wagons nor beasts of burden. And although they have no iron to cut these immense blocks, they are fitted to each other so perfectly that it is hard to put a point of a knife in the joints . . ."

The Spanish were amazed at what the Incas could make with only the simplest tools. The fortress of Cuzco still stands today on a hill behind the city. The largest blocks of stone weigh 200 tons. They were brought from more

The old Inca city of Macchu-Picchu, high in the mountains, was rediscovered in 1911. The building at the end of the street is called The Temple of the Three Windows. The Incas decorated the walls of their temples with golden images. These were in honor of the sun, which they worshiped as a god.

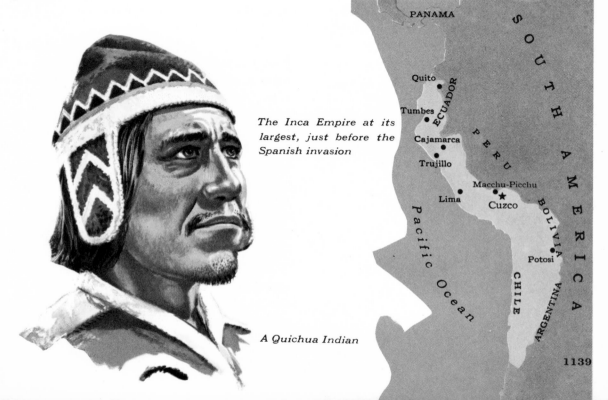

The Inca Empire at its largest, just before the Spanish invasion

PANAMA

SOUTH AMERICA

Quito

Tumbes
ECUADOR

Cajamarca
PERU

Trujillo

Macchu-Picchu
★
Lima   Cuzco

BOLIVIA

Pacific Ocean

Potosi

CHILE

ARGENTINA

A Quichua Indian

The Incas often built steps into their roads through the steep mountains.

than a mile away and were carved by workmen using stone tools. This building and others like it are proof of the skill of the Incas.

The Incas' skill is seen also in the remarkable system of roads that they built. The empire was so large that roads were tremendously important, particularly for sending messages. The Incas sent runners out on these roads to bring messages and orders to every point of the empire. The runners worked in relays, changing every mile, and a message could be taken as far as 150 miles in one day!

Of course the roads were also used for ordinary travel. At the time of the Spanish invasion the roads of the Incas ran through the Andes for thousands of miles. One of them connected Cuzco with Quito, 1,250 miles to the north.

Usually the roads were about 26 feet wide.

A raft made of balsa wood, with a sail (1) was used by the seafaring Incas. Boats made of cane (2) are still used today for fishing in the lakes.

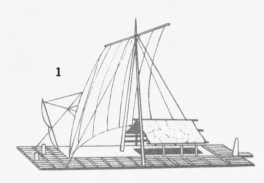

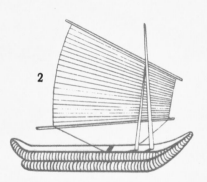

On the side of the mountain, people are working on one of the terraced farms.

They became narrower in the deep valleys and high mountains. Along steep cliffs, tunnels were built, wide enough for men and animals to pass through.

The Incas also utilized their engineering skill in constructing suspension bridges. These were made of five braided cables—three for the platform and two for the railing—slung from two stone towers. The bridges were so narrow that two people could not walk on them side by side.

The Incas were good farmers, too. They developed a method of terracing their land so that they could grow crops on the sides of the mountains. The most common crops were potatoes and corn. When the Spanish came to South America, they discovered these vegetables and took them back to Europe.

The Incas made ceramic vases and containers with great skill. Often they were elaborately decorated and colored. They could be hung by their handles on stone hooks.

urn   vase   vase   cup

The Incas also raised animals: guinea pigs for food, llamas for carrying burdens, and alpacas and vicunas for wool.

The power of the Incas came to an end with the Spanish invasion. But the Incas had built their roads and cities so well that many of them remain today. They are a constant reminder of the splendor of the Inca Empire hundreds of years ago.

The Incas raised vicunas, alpacas, llamas, and guinea pigs. Another animal used for food was the guanaco, a wild animal of the camel family.

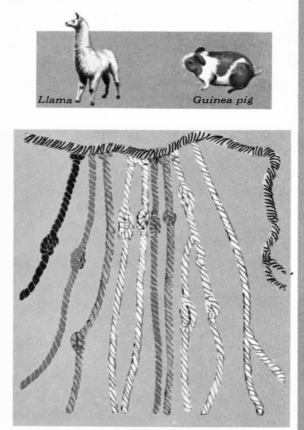

This device, called a quipu, was an Inca method of keeping records. Each color meant a person or thing. The knots indicated numbers. The government had a quipu for each citizen and it told everything about him—his products, his property, and how much he owed in taxes.

The Mighty Atom, Its Structure

Take a stick of wood that is one foot long and break it in two. Then take one of the six-inch pieces and break that in two. As you continue to divide the stick, you will have smaller and smaller pieces of wood—three inches, one and a half inches, three quarters of an inch, three eighths, and so on. In theory the pieces will become so small that you will no longer be able to see or cut them. But you can imagine breaking the wood into still smaller and smaller pieces.

One of the oldest questions of physics is concerned with this process of subdivision. Can we continue to break the stick indefinitely? Or will we eventually arrive at a particle—the atom— so small that it cannot be broken into anything else? The ancient Greeks were the first people we know of who tried to answer this question. In the fifth century B.C. the Greek philosopher Democritus proposed that all matter was composed of atoms. In Greek the word *atomos* means uncut, or something that cannot be divided. Democritus thought everything in the world was made up of atoms. However, other Greek thinkers, such as Aristotle, did not think this was true.

Strangely enough, both Democritus and his opponents were right. The world is made up of atoms. But the atoms themselves are made up of still smaller parts. To understand this, the atom must be studied.

An atom is the smallest complete particle of which an element—such as sodium or lead —is formed. An atom is so small, in fact, that it would take 250,000,000 of them to make a row one inch long.

WHAT THE ATOM IS MADE OF

An atom contains a nucleus composed of one or more positively charged particles called protons and neutral particles called neutrons. One or more negatively charged particles called electrons rotate around the nucleus.

The forces that keep electrons from flying off into space are complex. The most important

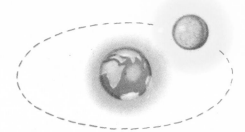

The hydrogen atom's one electron rotates about its nucleus as the moon rotates around the earth.

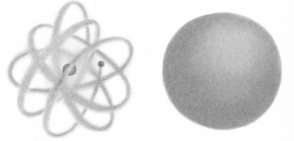

The electron moves so rapidly that it creates a shell about the nucleus.

reason the electrons stay in orbit is electrical attraction. Electrons are negatively charged, while protons are positively charged. In electricity, negative and positive charges attract each other. This electrical attraction keeps the electrons and the nucleus' protons together. Each atom is always electrically neutral, which means that the positive and negative charges— the protons and electrons—must always be equal in number.

The simplest atom to understand is the hydrogen atom because it has fewer parts than any other. The hydrogen atom has just one electron rotating about its nucleus, much as the moon turns about the earth. In one second the electron probably makes about 7,000,000,-000,000,000 rotations. Having just one electron, the hydrogen atom has just one proton in its nucleus.

In the atoms of the other elements the nuclei are not as simple. They have positive charges of two or more protons, and their protons are in turn balanced by two or more negatively charged electrons in orbit. If there are five protons in an atom, there will be five electrons, and so on. Also, every element except hydrogen has one or more neutrons in addition to the electrons and protons. The neutrons are

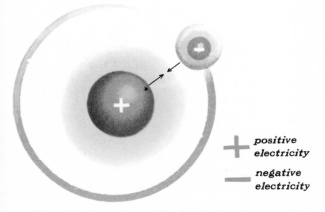

The central nucleus of the hydrogen atom consists of a single positively charged particle called a proton. A negatively charged electron rotates rapidly about the nucleus.

+ positive electricity

− negative electricity

Two protons are balanced by two electrons in the helium atom.

A carbon atom has six protons and six electrons.

Lithium has three electrons rotating about its three protons. Hence its atomic number is 3.

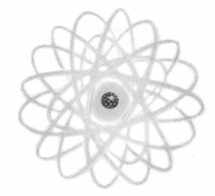

An iron atom has 26 protons and 26 electrons.

Four protons are balanced by four electrons in the beryllium atom.

A uranium atom has 92 protons and 92 electrons.

part of the nucleus along with the protons. A neutron has no electrical charge.

The atom of helium is the simplest next to hydrogen. It has two rotating electrons. In its nucleus it has two neutrons and two protons. Lithium, the next simplest, has three electrons in orbit and three protons and four neutrons in its nucleus. Uranium, one of the most complex atoms, has 92 protons, 92 electrons, and 146 neutrons.

ATOMIC NUMBER AND ATOMIC WEIGHT

The number of protons in any atom is referred to as the atomic number of that atom. Hydrogen's atomic number is 1 because it has one proton. The atomic number of helium is 2. Oxygen, with eight protons, is numbered 8, and uranium's number is 92. Besides having an atomic number, each atom has an atomic weight. This does not mean weight in grams or ounces, because such a figure would be so small as to be absurd. One atom of hydrogen, for example, weighs

$$\frac{1.6}{1,000,000,000,000,000,000,000,000}$$

of a gram. No physicist would want to work with complicated fractions like that, so a different unit of measurement was worked out. It is a unit that depends not on the actual weight of the atom, but on its relative weight—its weight compared to an atom of something else.

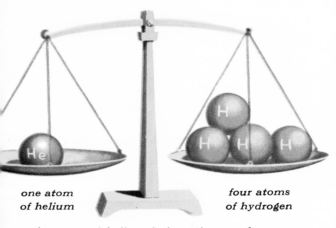

one atom
of helium

four atoms
of hydrogen

An atom of helium is four times as heavy as an atom of hydrogen.

The basic unit used in atomic weights is the atom of oxygen, which is regarded as weighing 16 units. Oxygen was chosen because it combines easily with many other elements, whose own atomic weights are thus readily calculated. Also, since an atom of oxygen weighs almost 16 times as much as an atom of hydrogen, this system enables us to give a value of one— 1.008, to be exact—for the atomic weight of hydrogen, the simplest of all atoms. This means that the atomic weight of an element shows how many times heavier its atom is than an atom of hydrogen. The atomic weight of helium is four. Its atom weighs as much as four hydrogen atoms.

There is a great deal of empty space between the central nucleus of an atom and the

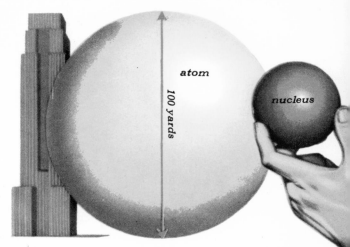

There is so much empty space inside an atom that if the atom could be magnified to a diameter of 100 yards, the nucleus would appear to be only the size of a billiard ball.

electrons. Since everything in the world is made of atoms, this means that everything, from the lightest feather to the heaviest automobile, is largely empty space dotted with nuclei and electrons. This does not mean that an atom is without weight or strength. If all the nuclei and electrons that make up a skyscraper were squeezed together, they would be no larger than a cherry stone. But the cherry stone would weigh 30,000 tons, the same weight as the skyscraper. There are some stars whose atoms are so tightly squeezed together that one matchbox full of their matter would weigh many hundreds of tons.

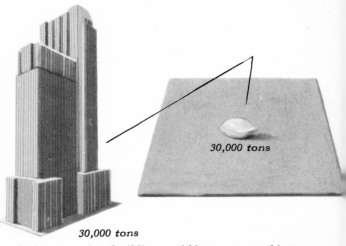

If the atoms in a building could be compressed into a very small space, the weight of the atoms would not change. It would remain the same.

Colonial America

From 1607, when the first permanent settlement was established at Jamestown, Virginia, colonists came to America from many different backgrounds and places. The early settlers in the South were mainly aristocratic Englishmen, intent on making money. New Netherlands was settled by wealthy Dutch who established landed estates. The middle colonies of New Jersey, Pennsylvania, and Delaware, as well as New England, were settled mainly by middle class people.

The English who settled New England were religious exiles, and they could expect little financial help from England. Those in the South came to make a profit, and they were more likely to import furniture, wives, and servants. The Dutch around New Amsterdam and the Germans and Swedes in Delaware and Pennsylvania brought with them the customs of their homelands.

As soon as possible the settlers built permanent houses, whose styles reflected the backgrounds of the people and the conditions of the particular colony or community.

The Puritans in New England cleared the trees from the land and built wooden houses. Because of the cold climate, most of the houses had deep cellars where food was stored below the frost line. The cellars had stone walls plastered with mud, and the chimneys were of stone. Dutch houses were built of brick and had steep tile roofs, like those in Holland. The favorite style of the German settlers was the solid fieldstone house, often built over a spring

Houses in New England had slanted roofs, covered with shingles. The small windows were covered with oiled paper or small, round panes of glass set in lead. The second story of the house often came out beyond the first story. If another room was needed, a lean-to was added at the back. This is called a salt-box type of house. Cooking was done over the fireplace. Meat was roasted on a spit. An iron crane hung inside the fireplace and pots were suspended from it. Ladder back chairs could be hung on the wall when not in use, and trundle beds fitted under the big beds.

The Dutch settlers built houses like the ones in Holland. They were made of brick with steep tile roofs. The brick sides at each end were often ornamented in a steplike pattern with black bricks set into the red to form a design. Because space in the homes was limited, settlers built long, narrow trestle tables and benches, chests for clothing, and beds built into corners or alcoves, concealed during the day by folding doors. Some colonists brought their own china with them. Later, pottery and glass were made. The New Netherlands colony lasted about 40 years.

so that its cellar could be used to cool milk. In the South colonists built brick plantation houses, with smaller cottages for the servants and field workers.

The early colonists hunted game in the forests until they had imported enough cattle, sheep, and pigs to provide meat. They raised corn for grain, and later rye and wheat. Food was sweetened with maple sugar, honey, or imported molasses or cane sugar. Salt was also imported. Since there was no refrigeration to preserve food, meat had to be smoked or salted, and corn and apples had to be dried.

New England farm products were consumed by the colonists there, but lumber and its products and fish were exported. In the Middle Colonies there was diversified agricul-

ture, and surplus wheat, flour, beef, and pork were exported, mainly to the West Indies. Maryland, Virginia, and North Carolina exported tobacco, and South Carolina and Georgia exported rice, indigo, and deerskins.

For baking, colonists built stone or brick ovens next to the fireplace and heated them with coals. Some baking was done in a bake kettle—a pot on legs with an iron lid. All the pots and kitchen utensils had very long handles so that they could reach across the fire in the fireplace, where most of the cooking was done.

The first settlers of Jamestown, New Amsterdam, and Plymouth brought with them only their household possessions. Before 1650 the colonies had woodworking craftsmen who made household furniture. All American furniture from about 1640 was the work of individual cabinetmakers. Cabinetmakers could be found, after 1675, in almost all colonial villages of any size.

At first a great many things were made at home. Clothes were made of flax or wool, which had to be carded, spun, and woven into cloth. Candles for lighting were hand dipped and made of sheep tallow or bayberry. For some candles, dry rushes were soaked in grease. There was also the betty lamp, a covered dish filled with grease, with a linen wick protruding from its lip. Soap, too, was made of grease, combined with lye extracted from wood ashes.

By 1700 crafts and industries had begun to grow, particularly in the New England and Middle Colonies. There were coopers who made barrels, tanners who cured leather, millers who ground grain, blacksmiths, pewterers, and later silversmiths. There were also cobblers, cordwainers, brickmakers, candlemakers, and clockmakers.

Travel between the colonies was mostly by river boats or coastal ships. Land travel was hard during most of the colonial period. At first there were few inns, and townspeople who had space were given licenses to offer rooms and food to travelers. Their homes were called ordinaries. Later, as more elaborate inns developed, their dining rooms and bars became social centers for the townspeople.

There was no regular mail in the early days of the colonies. People relied on travelers to carry letters to other towns. Since there were no street numbers, the address of the letter had to point out a landmark, such as a church or inn that was near the addressee's home. The first post office was established in Massachusetts in 1637. However, it wasn't until 1691 that a regular colonial post system was organized, with Andrew Hamilton the first postmaster general of America. By 1693 a regular post-rider service was established between the colonies. Post-riders carried newspapers as well as mail, and they collected the postage for a letter from the person to whom it was sent.

In the southern colonies, tobacco, rice, and other products requiring a good deal of land were grown, and the land was worked by slaves and indentured servants. The colonists built brick houses, along with small outlying cottages where the field workers and servants lived. Sometimes the kitchens were in a separate house and food was carried to the big house in covered dishes. The first dishes, which were called trenchers, were made of wood or pewter. Liquids were drunk from tankards made of pewter or leather. Spoons and knives were used, but not forks.

TIME CHART VOLUME 13 represents all time from the beginning of the earth to the present, which is calculated by most authorities to be four to six billion years. The lowest band covers a period of 1,000 years, counting back from the present to A.D. 1000. The band above it covers 4,000 years, counting back from the year A.D. 1000 to 5,000 years ago. Each band represents about four times as many years as the band directly below it. The third band covers 16,000 years, the one above it 64,000 years, and so on. As you go back in time, dates become more and more uncertain. Dates before recorded history—about 3000 B.C.—are the calculations and expert guesses of archeologists and geologists.

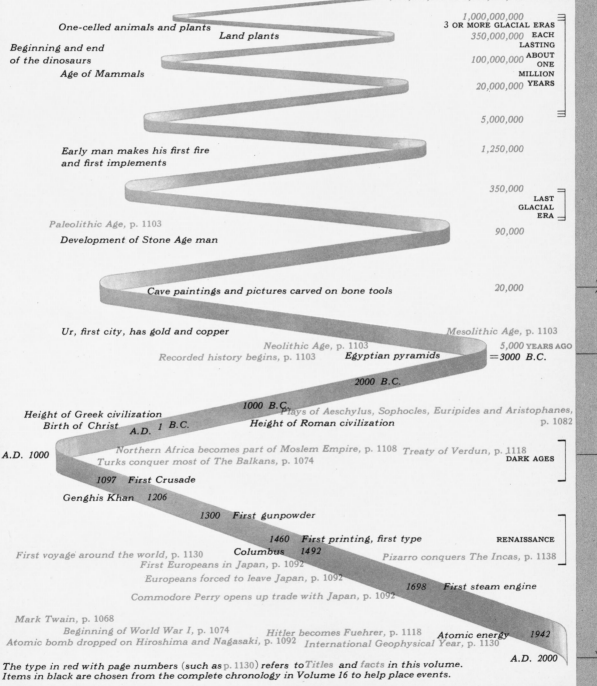

Oceans form and cool enough for first life

4,000,000,000 TO 6,000,000,000 YEARS AGO

One-celled animals and plants   Land plants
1,000,000,000
3 OR MORE GLACIAL ERAS
350,000,000 EACH
Beginning and end   LASTING
of the dinosaurs   100,000,000 ABOUT
Age of Mammals   ONE
                                            MILLION
20,000,000 YEARS

5,000,000

Early man makes his first fire   1,250,000
and first implements

350,000
LAST
GLACIAL
ERA
Paleolithic Age, p. 1103
Development of Stone Age man   90,000

Cave paintings and pictures carved on bone tools   20,000

Ur, first city, has gold and copper   Mesolithic Age, p. 1103

Neolithic Age, p. 1103   5,000 YEARS AGO
Recorded history begins, p. 1103   Egyptian pyramids   = 3000 B.C.

2000 B.C.

1000 B.C.   Plays of Aeschylus, Sophocles, Euripides and Aristophanes,
Height of Greek civilization   p. 1082
Birth of Christ   A.D. 1 B.C.   Height of Roman civilization

Northern Africa becomes part of Moslem Empire, p. 1108   Treaty of Verdun, p. 1118
A.D. 1000   Turks conquer most of The Balkans, p. 1074   DARK AGES

1097   First Crusade

Genghis Khan   1206

1300   First gunpowder

1460   First printing, first type   RENAISSANCE
First voyage around the world, p. 1130   Columbus   1492
First Europeans in Japan, p. 1092   Pizarro conquers The Incas, p. 1138

Europeans forced to leave Japan, p. 1092
1698   First steam engine
Commodore Perry opens up trade with Japan, p. 1092

Mark Twain, p. 1068
Beginning of World War I, p. 1074   Hitler becomes Fuehrer, p. 1118   Atomic energy   1942
Atomic bomb dropped on Hiroshima and Nagasaki, p. 1092   International Geophysical Year, p. 1130
A.D. 2000

EACH BAND COVERS FOUR TIMES AS MANY YEARS AS THE BAND BELOW IT

16,000 YEARS   4,000 YEARS   1,000 YEARS

The type in red with page numbers (such as p. 1130) refers to Titles and facts in this volume.
Items in black are chosen from the complete chronology in Volume 16 to help place events.